HOLY HOTBED

Transgenerational Trauma Transmission
in the
Israeli-Palestinian Conflict

BURNING BRIDGE
PUBLISHING

HOLY HOTBED

Transgenerational Trauma Transmission
in the
Israeli-Palestinian Conflict

Danger Geist

www.BurningBridge.com

Book art and cover designed by Trevor Niemann
Burning Bridge Publishing logo designed by Ryan Rizzio

www.BurningBridge.com

Printed in the United States of America.

1st edition, January 2020

Publisher's Cataloging-in-Publication Data

Names: Geist, Danger, author.
Title: Holy hotbed : transgenerational trauma transmission in the Israeli-Palestinian conflict / Danger Geist.
Description: 1st edition. | Tulsa, OK : Burning Bridge Publishing, 2020. | Includes bibliographical references and index.
Identifiers: LCCN 2020901509 (print) | ISBN 978-1-937691-07-3 (paperback) | ISBN 978-1-937691-08-0 (ebook : Kindle) | ISBN 978-1-937691-09-7 (ebook)
Subjects: LCSH: Arab-Israeli conflict--Psychological aspects. | Jewish-Arab relations--Psychological aspects. | Psychic trauma. | Psychology--Research. | Eschatology. | BISAC: PSYCHOLOGY / Research & Methodology. | RELIGION / Eschatology.
Classification: LCC DS134 .G45 2020 (print) | LCC DS134 (ebook) | DDC 956.94--dc23.

Dedication

I dedicate this project to my beloved Romy girl. I promised that this lifestyle was only temporary, and that more-attentive days were ahead. Instead, this life was the only thing I ever offered you. I hope I loved enough before, and I hope you know I love you forever.

🐾

Abstract

A phenomenological research study was conducted to assess the impact of Transgenerational Trauma Transmission (TTT) in Israelis and Palestinians who live amidst the Israeli-Palestinian Conflict. The history of the Israeli-Palestinian Conflict and the Israeli (Jewish) and Palestinian (Muslim) eschatological viewpoints were also investigated for impact. Ten Israeli adults in Jerusalem and seven Palestinian adults throughout the West Bank ($N = 17$) between the ages of 18 and 35 participated in hour-long qualitative interviews with questions that assessed TTT and religious/eschatological beliefs. After collection and data analysis that included NVivo, seven themes were identified among the participants: (a) those dealing with TTT do not recognize their trauma as clinically significant; (b) those dealing with TTT display behavioral changes and negative somatic manifestations rather than psychological symptoms; (c) those dealing with TTT have loss of faith; (d) those dealing with TTT have relational barriers with those belonging to the group that their elders have had conflict with; (e) those dealing with TTT do not necessarily hate those belonging to the group that their elders have had conflict with; (f) Israelis and Palestinians have contempt for the conflict and resentment towards those in authority who exacerbate the conflict; and (g) Israelis and Palestinians do not believe there is a solution to the conflict that does not involve war. This study prompted three takeaways for future research: (1) there needs to be a stronger distinction between Israelis/Palestinians' settlement, educational, and military experiences; (2) physical manifestations of trauma ought to be assessed as fully as mental symptoms; and (3) psychosocial gaps should be examined in regards to both the individual participant as well as the participant's immediate community environment.

Keywords: transgenerational trauma, trauma transference, eschatology, Israeli-Palestinian Conflict.

TABLE OF CONTENTS

A quick reference index can be found on the last page.

Chapter 1: Nature of the Study

Background

If you are American, Cuban, Rwandan, Angolan, Russian, Italian, Ghanaian, Argentinian, Ukrainian, Armenian, Algerian, Australian, Korean, Japanese, Lebanese, Chinese, Sudanese, Taiwanese, Irish, Swedish, Spanish, Polish, Tajikistani, Iraqi, Pakistani, Kazakhstani, Saudi, Virgin Islander, Dutch, Filipino, Kyrgyz, Icelandic, or Belizean and your people are the subject of a systematic termination, then you are suffering from a genocide, execution, extermination, annihilation, decimation, massacre, slaughter, mass murder, or ethnic cleansing. But only if you are a Jew can you be the subject of a pogrom. No other ethnic population has been the victim of violence so frequently and so intensely that there exists a vocabulary word that was created to describe genocide against this specific people (Astashkevich, 2018; Bartová, 2016; Aronson, 1980).

The Jewish race and religion is interlinked with longsuffering, and this identity has become a factor in each of its modern-day conflicts (Schori-Eyal, Halperin, & Bar-Tal, 2014). Unlike most other ethnic conflicts, the Israeli-Palestinian Conflict has a unique component in that ethnic identity is tertiary in comparison to the religious and territorial components of the conflict. Rydelnik (2007) and Brueggemann (2015) explored the complicated background of the Israeli-Palestinian conflict from a religious perspective in which they highlighted the failure to compromise in every effort over the past 60 years. While Rydelnik's (2007) biases lean towards favoring Israel and Brueggeman's (2015) conversely makes an argument for Palestinians, both agree on this point that compromise has never worked.

As a result of this ongoing conflict, countless Israelis and Palestinians are killed every year, including children who do not have (or want any part in) the conflict. The conflict has been a political pressure point since Israel claimed its independence in 1948 and continues to be a controversial topic today. The Israeli-Palestinian conflict is so nuanced that a cross-cultural perspective is incompatible as there are no other modern conflicts that it can be compared against.

As such, a cultural relativist approach is necessary, and internal validity is favored over external validity (Van de Vijver et al., 2011).

Cole and Hatano (2010) have emphasized that cultural psychology brings the assumption that all human processes are the result of culture. That is to say, the development of historical culture unabashedly affects psychological processes throughout humanity. Cole and Hatano described a particular cultural mediation in which material objects are modified to become culturally relevant. Thus, the physical world – even an inanimate object – can regulate psychological processes. In fact, this is the entire supposed premise of the Israeli-Palestinian conflict. At its core, the conflict is about land (Frantzman & Kark, 2013; Ben-Dror & Ziedler, 2015; Rydelnik, 2007; Films for Action, 2009). But as Cole and Hatano (2010) have identified, the land represents something much more important than infertile soil.

One likely representation is that the land represents the collective memory of its people. Hirsch (1997) has discussed the concept of postmemory in which trauma can be passed down intergenerationally. Steir-Livny (2016) expounded upon Hirsch's research and emphasized that Israelis have actually been victims in the past (i.e., the Holocaust), even if they are not currently in that category of necessarily being victims. As such, Steir-Livny argued, reconciliation is more critical than discussions about disputed land.

There is also a significant gap in the current literature in terms of analyzing the Israeli-Palestinian conflict from a religious lens. Specifically, Jews tend to believe they are God's chosen people and have a right to all of the land in that area; Muslims tend to believe the Jews are wrong, and that Muslims deserve the land; Christians believe in the Bible, which clearly asserts that Jews were given that land by God (Rydelnik, 2007). Most Israelis are Jews, most Palestinians are Muslims, and the Christian perspective has long affected the American policy of considering Israel as an ally (Cole & Hatano, 2010). Jews, Christians, and Muslims alike believe in an eschatological prophecy in which a leader named Gog leads his group of nations, Magog, into battle against Israel (Dittmer, 2007; Shenk, 2007). In all three faith traditions, Magog is largely comprised of Arab nations, and the focus

2

of their attack is on the Jews in Israel. In Judaism and Christianity, the Jews conquer Gog and Magog (Rydelnik, 2007); in Islam, Gog and Magog prevail and eradicate Israel and its Jews (Zuhur et al., 2008).

An individual's religious beliefs affects their psychological processes and ultimately their behaviors (Regnerus & Uecker, 2007; Wyshak, 2016; Heim & Schaal, 2014; Koenig et al., 2017). It is not a stretch, then, to think that a religious adherent might have a staunch political stance that also reflects their religion's eschatological views, and Shenk (2007) notes that Islamic apocalyptic literature has substantially increased since the formation of the State of Israel because "God commands justice; the State of Israel is founded on injustice and therefore must be dismantled" (p. 120). Despite this, when searching for peer-reviewed data with the combined keywords "eschatology" and "psychology" on EBSCO Host, only 248 hits were returned, and most of the articles were unrelated to any component of the Israeli-Palestinian Conflict or equated eschatology with extremism. However, eschatological viewpoints are also common for moderate religious adherents of Islam (Shenk, 2007) and Christians alike (Brueggemann, 2015; Woodridge, 2006). The prophecy of Gog and Magog is found in all three of the Abrahamic religions' core holy texts, but when the keywords "eschatology," "psychology," and "Magog" were entered into EBSCO Host, only one article was identified as a match. The one peer-reviewed article described an 18th-century Englishwoman named Joanna Southcott (1750-1814) who claimed that an eschatological battle was imminent, and that despite being a virgin and 64 years old, she was pregnant with the second (and final) manifestation of Christ (Holloway, 2015). Seventeen doctors evaluated her claims, and all 17 agreed that she was pregnant, but Southcott died before she ever gave birth. Upon autopsy, there was no indication that she had been pregnant, but this strange set of circumstances was enough to launch the Southcottian Movement, which views political matters through this eschatological prophecy and still has adherents today.

If the obscure Joanna Southcott was able to launch an eschatological-political religious movement, then how much more might Jesus, Mohammad, or Ezekiel. In fact, it was Iranian President Ahmadinejad who wrote to U.S. President George W. Bush in 2006,

3

appealing to Bush's Christian beliefs so that they might have a dialogue about political matters in light of their respective religious prophecies (Shenk, 2007). Yet, the field of psychology has long tried to establish itself as a firm science in the face of its skeptics, and the inclusion of religious discussions in psychological literature – especially regarding eschatological topics – are often eschewed out of fear that faith-based analyses might render the field of psychology as a pseudoscience. Yet, religion has played a role in nearly every aspect of the Israeli-Palestinian Conflict.

Consider the history of the al-Aqsa Mosque: though only the third holiest site (behind Mecca and Medina respectively), Muslims fiercely contend that the Temple Mount that al-Aqsa lies on should be under their control – not Jews' or Christians', whom revere the site with even more religious significance than their Muslim counterparts (Molloy, 2013). For Muslims, it is where their prophet ascended into heaven; for Jews, it is literally the location where the Messianic Age is to be birthed as the Third Temple is built there; for Christians, that Third Temple's desecration heralds in the second coming of Christ (Shenk, 2007). The plot of land debatably pales in significance compared to its extreme importance in Judaism and Christianity, but Shenk argues that one reason Muslims care so much to defend the location is because it is not only their way to protect their eschatological narrative but to also prevent the Christians' and Jews' narrative.

Or consider the history of Jerusalem's Eastern Gate: of the eight gates leading into the Old City of Jerusalem, it is the only one that is sealed shut. Breaking this seal would be an immense help logistically (as the Temple Mount is just on the other side), but the impact of religion prevents this: in Isaiah 63 of the Hebrew Scriptures, a prophecy is foretold that the Messiah will come from the east into Jerusalem, presumably through the Eastern Gate. Zechariah 14:4 similarly reads that the Messiah will come through the Eastern Gate to be presented as king. As a result of these prophecies, Sultan Suleiman of the Ottoman Empire had the Eastern Gate sealed shut in 1541 with sixteen feet of concrete so that the Messiah could not physically pass through this gate (Morgenstern, 1929; Got Questions, 2018; Gomby, 2017). Additionally, a Muslim cemetery was erected at its site so that even if a Jewish Messiah could break through the seal, he would not use the gate because rabbinical law cites that entering a cemetery would result in the individual becoming defiled (Magdalene Publishing, 2018). However, it would seem the sultan was over 1500 years belated as Christian apocryphal texts credit the Eastern Gate as the one that Jesus passed through on Palm Sunday (Gomby, 2017).

The sultan's attempt to thwart Jewish prophecy ironically fulfilled another one in Ezekiel 44 that predicted that this gate would one day be sealed (Got Questions, 2018). CBN Israel (2017) and Clinton (2013) both describe an anecdote that during the Six-Day War in 1967, the Jewish military devised a strategy to blow up the Eastern Gate so they could launch a surprise flank on the Palestinians from the east, but an Orthodox Jew decried the military strategy as blasphemy and convinced the Jewish soldiers that their holy scriptures make it clear that only the Messiah should ever pass through the gate again.

I am convinced that for as long as the Eastern Gate remains sealed, religion has a place in scientific literature. The Eastern Gate prophecy has driven policy for hundreds of years, but exactly zero scholarly articles are returned by EBSCO Host when a search for this topic is conducted. Only Google Scholar produced a single peer-reviewed article, albeit from 1929. As a result, researchers who want to study this topic are confined to using either individual conversations with religious adherents or using non-scholarly sources like the Christian Broadcasting Network, Magdalene Publishing, or GotQuestions.org, all of which clearly identify themselves as Christian ministries. It seems like a curious approach to intentionally scrape this construct that has impacted Jerusalem's politics for thousands of years, even circumventing practical military strategy.

Further, Christian and Muslim adherents pray daily for their apocalyptic prophecies to come true: Muslims repeat the Fatiha 16 times every day with their face on the ground as part of their Salaat, asking Allah for favor on the day of judgment; Christians frequently pray "Thy kingdom come, thy will be done on earth as it is in heaven" (Shenk, 2007, p. 123). Shenk describes the Christian church as an "eschatological community pressing forward toward the day when the kingdom of God will be fulfilled" (p. 121), and he notes that Muslims similarly are eschatologically-focused.

Yet, there is a significant gap in research in the way religious eschatology has affected the conflict. Few scholarly articles address the eschatological aspect of the Battle of Gog and Magog, a battle that is an unfulfilled prophecy in each of the three Abrahamic religions (Shenk, 2007). In Christianity, the battle precedes the Second Coming of Jesus Christ; in Judaism, the battle precedes the arrival of the Messiah; in Islam, the battle precedes the heavenly descension of the "last Mahdi" and Jesus of Nazareth (Molloy, 2013). All three interpretations of the battle agree on one thing: it will usher in the last days of earth. For most Christians (and particularly postmillennial dispensationalists), this means Christ's final judgment is at hand; for Jews, the Messianic Age has arrived; for Muslims, the Last Mahdi and Jesus destroy non-Muslims and heavenly angels to establish Islam as the one true religion (Dittmer, 2007; Woodridge, 2006; Shenk, 2009; Zuhur et al., 2008; Bisel & Ford, 2008; Murray & O'Driscoll, 1997; Rydelnik, 2007; Geist, 2012). Meanwhile, Jews and Christians believe that a battle is coming, at which time God's chosen people (i.e., Israel) will defeat the region of "Magog" which most historians see as the Commonwealth of Independent States (formerly southern USSR), Iran, and Turkey (Dittmer, 2007; Rydelnik, 2007). Despite the interfaith belief in this coming battle, there is somehow almost no research on this eschatological topic. It is difficult to handle such a sensitive religious issue in an appropriate and empirical way, so it makes sense that few have discussed this issue. However, it is an issue that demands consideration as the conflict cannot be fully discussed without an understanding of the way the prophesied battle-to-come plays into the conflict.

Finally, it needs to be noted that any discussion of the Israeli-Palestinian conflict is a complex and highly emotional one in which researchers across countless years have been trying to find a solution for peace. It would be arrogant to assume any individual study could add much more to the discussion. Instead, the hope is that this research will provide better understanding on just one of the many facets that make up the conflict.

The History of the Conflict

If only given one sentence to summate the entire Israeli-Palestinian Conflict, it would be this: "Israelis and Palestinians do not operate off of the same historical facts as one another, and they are instead engaged in a war of differing narratives, which are informed by ancient religious texts and ethnic traditions that have spanned millennia." (Technically a run-on sentence, but it counts.)

If allotted a few sentences, I would add these specific details: "In 1948 during the midst of the aftermath of the Holocaust, the United Nations offered the land of Israel – which was colonized by the British at the time – as a safe haven for Jews. However, this land was concurrently settled by Palestinians who refused to concede the land, resulting in a violent war that same year between the Palestinians and the newly-settled Israelis. The State of Israel quelled the uprising and hundreds of thousands of Palestinians were exiled. In 1967, Palestinians collaborated with nearby Arab nations and launched a strategic offensive to take the land back. The Arab nations ultimately failed and lost even more land in the process. Specifically, Israelis suppressed the offensive in six days and took control of the West Bank, the Gaza Strip, the Golan Heights, and much of the Sinai Peninsula. In the years after the 1967 war, Palestinians conceded to Israelis that they would let them have the land as established by the UN in 1948, but only if they returned the land that they took control of in 1967. Israel refused to willingly hand over the land, citing that the 1948 borders left them tactically vulnerable, as evidenced by the 1967 Palestinian offensive. Since then, Israelis and Palestinians have remained in conflict, with Palestinians organizing sporadic uprisings against Israel, while Israelis build settlements in Palestinian territory. Several peace treaties have been attempted, of which usually include concession of land by Israel and a collective acknowledgement by Palestine of Israel's right to exist. Exactly zero of these treaties have worked. Why is that? Please see the previous paragraph's run-on sentence."

However, if I was given 20 or 25 pages to summarize the Israeli-Palestinian Conflict, it would probably look like this:

7

The Arab-Israeli Conflict

In its first 50 years of existence, the State of Israel participated in seven wars (Katz & Lavee, 2004). Yet, the Israeli-Palestinian Conflict is only a smaller chapter of the larger narrative that is the Arab-Israeli Conflict, which did not fully manifest until the 1948 War – the same year Israel achieved independence. Modern Israel is 99% made up of Israelis and Arabs (see Table 1).

TABLE 1: Basic demographics of Israel (Katz & Lavee, 2004)*
*does not include Palestinian figures

Ethnicity	Percentage
Jewish	78% > 40% European-American immigrants > 33.5% Asian-American immigrants > 26.5% natural-born Israelis
Arab	21% > 75% Muslim descent > 16% Christian descent > 9% Druze/mixed/other
Other	≈ 1%

The land that is known as Israel today has gone through countless possessions of different ethnic groups, empires, and dynasties. Jews have tried to maintain control of the land long Before Christ (B.C.), and the Arab-Israeli struggle for control of the land is arguably the longest-lasting conflict in the history of the world. For most of the modern era, neither the Jews nor Palestinians had control of the land as it belonged to the Ottoman Empire, but in 1840 at the Convention of London, the Ottoman Empire agreed to a peace treaty that included a provision that they would share the land with Palestinian Arabs in an attempt to quell incessant uprisings (Nets-Zehngut, 2014).

In the late 1800s, Jewish Zionists appeared in Israel during the reign of the Ottoman Empire to reclaim their land (Nets-Zehngut, 2014). As more Jews continued to migrate to Palestinian land, Palestinian nationalism rose. As Palestinian nationalism rose, so did ethnic tension, followed by the inevitable violence. Despite the fact that the Palestinians yet greatly outnumbered the Jews, there was concern from Palestinians that they were losing control of their land.

During World War I, what became known as the "McMahon-Hussein Correspondence" took place in which Sir Henry McMahon, the British High Commissioner, requested the help of Arabs to defeat the Ottoman Empire, offering the promise of an independent state of Palestine as a dangling carrot. Hussein bin Ali, the Sharif of Mecca, agreed to help the British with the aid of his Arab army, and the Ottoman Empire was quickly put down (Staub, 2013; Jhally, Alper, & Earp, 2016; Frantzman & Kark, 2013). History would hold that the British were making promises they did not intend to keep, though, as the British had also declared their intent to give this same land to the Jewish people in the 1917 Balfour Declaration (Schwanitz, 2018; Staub, 2013).

Of course, unfavorable views towards the Jews in the late 1800s and early 1900s were not unique to the Palestinians. By the time the Third Reich came into power, anti-Semitism was abound throughout the world (Brustein, 2003). During World War II, negotiations for an allotment of Jewish land was far from the top concern for Jews around the world who were scraping by just to avoid being thrown in a Nazi Concentration Camp.

When Nazi Germany fell and post-war assessments were made, the loss of life within the Jewish community was staggering: the world was shocked to find that millions of Jews had been killed – most executed in brutal fashion – during the course of the war (Lipstadt, 1993). The need for a designated national land for Jews was never clearer, and as a result, the United Nations (in conjunction with British approval) declared in 1948 that part of the Palestinian land currently owned by the British would become the Sovereign State of Israel (Ben-Dror & Ziedler, 2015).

The 1948 War

The 1948 United Nations resolution, in which the land previously controlled by the Ottoman Empire was handed over from the British to the Jews, was not well-received by Palestinians who claimed that they were the rightful heirs of the land (Nets-Zehngut, 2014). This disagreement led to the 1948 War between the Arabs and the newly-minted Israelis. Still feeling the sting from World War II and, specifically, the effects of the Holocaust, the United Nations stood by Israel as the rightful owners of the land. This, in combination with the Jews defeating the Arabs in the 1948 War, led to half the Palestinian population being displaced – more than a half-million Arabs (Sabatinelli et al., 2009). Today, over 5 million Palestinians are displaced refugees as a result of the 1948 War (Jhally, Alper, & Earp, 2016; Seita & Shaikh, 2013). While the *Shoah* – which is the Jewish word for "Holocaust" – was catastrophic for the Jews, the tragedy ultimately encumbered Palestinians, too. For every negative connotation that Jews associate with the word "Shoah," so do the Palestinians have a similarly oppugnant word that designates their misery: *Nakba*, as the 1948 displacement became known, literally means "disaster" or "catastrophe" in Arabic (Sen, 2015). Phyllis Bennis of the Institute for Policy Studies aptly states about Palestinians, "They were not the Nazis. They were not responsible for the Holocaust, but they were the ones who paid the price" (Omeish & Omeish, 2006).

Of course, this very friction is a critical part of the Israeli-Palestinian Conflict today: Palestinians believe that they should be returned to their homeland. However, there are many millions more Palestinians today than there were in 1948, and (as the Israelis argue), allowing such a sheer number of Palestinians back into what had previously been their land would lead to a dangerously disproportionate number of Palestinians in the Israeli territory. In fact, in a survey of refugees conducted in Tel Aviv in 2010, 91% of the Jews sampled indicated that they believed they would be exterminated if Palestinians were allowed back into the land (Nets-Zehngut, 2014).

Adding to the complexity, there is debate regarding whether the Palestinians left willingly after the 1948 War or if they were forced to leave (Sabatinelli et al., 2009; Seita & Shaikh, 2013; Ben-Dror & Ziedler, 2015; Brueggemann, 2015). The Jewish collective memory is that the Palestinians, reeling from their loss, willingly gave up their land in 1948. Conversely, the Arab collective memory is that the Palestinians were expelled by the government of Israel. Scholars argue that the truth is probably somewhere between the two extreme viewpoints, though even that cannot be certain due to so much conflicting information.

Regardless, these collective memories have since affected the way Israelis and Palestinians interact. Why would an Israeli who was raised to believe that the Palestinians left willingly after the loss of a war ever concede that land to Palestinians? Many of the Palestinian collective memories assert that the Holocaust, at best, has been overblown to pit the Jews as victims (Kellerman, 2001) and, at worst, never happened at all (Steir-Livny, 2016). For a Jew who has the collective memory that the Jews deserved and were imparted their land by UN mandate and Palestinian defeat, the logical option is to oppose Palestinians who have a differing collective memory. Such issues are at the heart of this Israeli-Palestinian Conflict, and drive the distrust between the two ethnicities today.

The Israeli-Palestinian Tension: 1948 – 1967

While Israelis remained in warfare after the 1948 War, the Israeli-Palestinian Conflict actually salved to a cool, if perhaps only because the Palestinians and Israelis were no longer sharing the same space anymore. After 1948, most Palestinians had retreated to Jordan and remained neutral in any conflicts involving Israel. Still, every attempt for a semblance of peace between Israelis and Arabs during that period resulted in nothing but greater bloodshed (Zilkha, 1992). Arabs built up their military forces and, in May 1967, Israel's borders were surrounded by an Arab coalition that included Egypt and Syria. The Arab coalition, led by Egyptian President Gamal Abdel Nasser, boasted 250,000 soldiers, 2,000 tanks, and 700 aircraft. Nasser declared "our basic objective will be to destroy Israel" (Zilkha, 1992, p. 31). 10 days later on June 5, 1967, Israel launched a pre-emptive offensive against the Arab coalition advancing towards them, sparking the Six-Day War.

The First Three Days of The Six-Day War: June 5 to 7, 1967

Israel entered the Six-Day War in want of support. The United States, who had long supported the establishment and development of Israel, was not officially an ally of Israel and were not willing to support Israel's efforts (CBN Israel, 2017). Even France, Israel's one official ally, abandoned their alliance the night before the Six-Day War, having condemned Israel's pre-emptive strike. Additionally, France imposed an arms embargo on the Middle East, which they knew would significantly hurt Israel if war were to break out. War did break out, and Israel was without any support (Bass, 2010).

Despite their solitude, Israel attacked swiftly and efficiently: following an airstrike that proved catastrophic to Egyptian forces, Israeli forces pushed through to the Gaza Strip and Sinai, eventually reaching the Suez Canal (Zilkha, 1992). To this point, Palestinians had not joined in the engagement. However, after the capture of the Suez Canal, the king of Jordan joined the Arab coalition in their efforts to destroy Israel, citing moral duty and an Arab pact. The Jordanian army launched massive offensives against eastern Israel and Tel Aviv. However, Israel had anticipated that Jordan may eventually jump off the sidelines during the battle and had prepared a contingency plan for such a circumstance. Israel was able to not only push Jordanian forces back, but essentially obliterated the entire Jordanian air force and captured the Old City Jerusalem, including the Jews' holiest site: the Western Wall. While the Jordanian king appeared on Jordanian and Palestinian televisions begging them to fight Jews "to the last drop of blood" (Zilkha, 1992, p. 32), he accepted a ceasefire by the end of that same day despite having lost Palestinian land to Israel.

The Last Three Days of The Six-Day War: June 9 to 11, 1967

With the threat of the Egyptians and Jordanians extinguished, the Israelis focused their efforts on the Syrians in Golan Heights. The Israelis – knowing that Syria no longer had air cover following a Syrian loss of their air force during a raid in Haifa – devised a plan to destroy the rest of the Syrian forces. Between June 9th and 10th, some Israeli forces pushed through on the ground while other Israeli forces "rushed to climb hundreds of feet of steep terrain under heavy fire to dislodge the Syrians from their fortifications" (Zilkha, 1992, p. 33). The mountain division of Israeli forces sustained heavy casualties, but did eventually make it to the top of the Golan Heights plateau. The Israeli forces prepared themselves for a counterattack that never materialized. Instead, many of the Syrian commanders had retreated, and Syrian soldiers burned military documents and blew up their own bunkers in surrender. When the Israeli forces reached the Syrian stronghold on June 10th, they found it abandoned. Even perfectly-working tanks had been left behind in the Syrian retreat. By June 11th, the UN had brokered a ceasefire for the Six-Day War, which had largely ended in Israeli victory the day previously.

June 1967 to The First Intifada

In a matter of less than a week, Israel had destroyed the armies from Egypt, Syria, and Jordan, claiming East Jerusalem, the West Bank, the Gaza Strip, Sinai, and Golan Heights (Zilkha, 1992). Israel had not only defended its own land from capture, but captured all of Palestine as well. In 1979, Israel and Egypt came to a peace treaty in which Israel promised to return the Sinai Plateau back to Egypt in exchange for Egypt's recognition of Israel as a sovereign state. Egypt agreed, and by 1982, Israel had completely pulled from Sinai, returning it to Egyptian control.

However, in this same year, Israel orchestrated a military invasion into Lebanon for more land. The global community denounced the invasion as imperialistic and bullish. Even the conservative media outlets in the United States referred to the event as the "Massacre in Lebanon" and condemned Israel's denial of the violence in the face of clear video evidence, which put tension on U.S.-Israeli ties (Jhally, Alper, & Earp, 2016).

Israel immediately recognized its new perception as "bullies" and instigated a public relations campaign known as *Hasbara*. The word itself means "to explain" in Hebrew, and has since developed into a campaign that exists even today to "create a positive image" of Israel (Jhally, Alper, & Earp, 2016). At one early conference discussing the Hasbara campaign, an Israeli noted that "Israel is no longer perceived to be 'little David' but Goliath steamrolling across the map" (Jhally, Alper, & Earp, 2016). As a means to conduct damage control on its image, the campaign hired Carl Spielvogel who was responsible for helping Miller Lite rebrand itself in 1979 from being a "girl's beer" to a "tough guy's beer" that was a less-filling and better-tasting alternative to the other light beers out there. In addition to Spielvogel, right-wing political consultant Frank Luntz was hired to change the Israeli-Palestinian Conflict narrative from being about "territory" to one about "terror" (Jhally, Alper, & Earp, 2016). That is, as long as the American media portrayed Palestinians as being more concerned with committing terror (rather than the real issues of land dispute), the hearts and minds of the American people would side with Israel over Palestine.

Israel successfully rebranded itself after its 1982 misstep in Lebanon, but no such success was similarly achieved in Israeli-Palestinian attempts for peace. Countless efforts have been attempted for the following exchange: land from the Israelis, peace and acknowledgement from Palestinians. All efforts have failed for complicated reasons. In short, Palestinians wanted the Israeli borders to be what they were on June 5, 1967 (i.e., before Israel captured Palestine in the Six-Day War). Israel's position has been that returning to 1948 borders (as opposed to 1967 borders) threatens Israel's right to existence, attributing many of the offensives launched against them to have taken place (in part) because the 1948 borders allowed for advantageous military positions against Israel. Keeping the borders as they have been since 1967 is an issue that Israel believes to be a matter of self-preservation. Due to an unwillingness to forfeit the land (namely, the West Bank and the Gaza Strip) that was captured in 1967, Palestinians attempted the First Intifada: an uprising to take back the West Bank and Gaza Strip by force.

Hamas & the First Intifada: 1987-2000

By the 20th anniversary of the Six-Day War, tension between Palestinians and Israelis hit an all-time high. There were many reports of violence between Israelis and Palestinians, though each of these instances were chalked up to rogue individuals and not the work of the government. This changed in December 1987, when an Israeli military vehicle collided with a civilian Palestinian vehicle, killing four

Palestinian passengers and injuring ten. The Israeli military claimed it was an accident, but Gaza Palestinians were certain that it was a deliberate act (Aziza, 2017). The First Intifada began as an act of civil disobedience that included boycotts of Jewish businesses, but quickly erupted into a scene of Israeli soldiers shooting Palestinians who were throwing Molotov cocktails. By the end of 1988, Israel had deployed 80,000 soldiers and over 300 Palestinians were killed – at least 50 of whom were children.

In the first year of the uprising, Egyptian Sheikh Ahmed Yassin founded the Islamic Resistance Movement, a grassroots humanitarian organization that was focused on Palestinian social work, especially offering free medical services to Gaza Palestinians who had been wounded by Israelis during this time period. The organization was based upon Sunni Islam, of which Sheikh Yassin was a well-known mullah. The full name of the Islamic Resistance Movement in Arabic is "Harakat Al-Muqawama Al-Islamia," which came to be known by its acronym, H.A.M.A.S. Ironically, the Arabic word "Hamas" actually means "violence" or "zeal" (Cepoi, 2013). However, while contemporary Israelis associate Hamas with terrorism, this was not always the case. When Hamas was established in 1987, it was known for its community service, namely for building and managing schools, orphanages, mosques, and sports facilities. They were well-beloved by Gaza Palestinians, and even many Israelis supported the movement (Cepoi, 2013). For the Israelis, Hamas initially appeared as a contrast to the violent Fatah movement, the terrorist cell led by Yasser Arafat (who had been Public Enemy No. 1 to the Jewish people at the time). Hamas embraced this image, presenting itself as a nonviolent alternative to the Palestine Liberation Organization.

However, the relationship between Hamas and Israel quickly grew sour. The Palestinian resistance that began in 1987 – coined as the "Intifada" or "uprising" at the time, and later referred to as "The First Intifada" – had escalated, and Hamas began participating in its events. In 1988, Hamas released a charter which condemned any politician who seeks to make peace with Israel as standing in the way of Allah (Robinson, 2007). In 1989, Hamas committed its first attack against the Israeli military, and Hamas's leader, Sheikh Yassin, was convicted of orchestrating the kidnapping and execution of two Israeli soldiers (Cepoi, 2013; Israel Ministry of Foreign Affairs, 2004). Initially funded by Saudi Arabia, guerrilla fighters emerged, armed with guns, rockets, and the technical expertise to create bombs. During the uprising, the United States declared its support for Israel, and Hamas subsequently established itself as an opponent of the United States and began sponsoring suicide bombings against Israeli civilians and military. Yet, Hamas has taken offense at being considered a terrorist organization. Zuhur et al. write of Hamas's peaceful intent for the Brotherhood of Muslims:

> Like all Ilkwhan [Muslim Brothers], they accept any Muslim who calls himself or herself a Muslim. In other words, they are not a Takfirist group. They are not like al-Qaeda; they are not like the Daghmoush-led Islamic army in Gaza and some smaller groups. They do aim for consensus; they do have and have always had a democratic process in their organization intended to inhibit factionalism. They are pragmatic. They have avoided conflict whenever possible with countries other than Israel. (Zuhur et al., 2008, p. 2)

Hamas was not intended as a terror cell; the overarching purpose of Hamas has been to raise the Islam banner everywhere possible, partially in anticipation for the upcoming prophesied Battle of Gog and Magog, in which Muslims believe Allah will destroy Israel in due time (Zuhur et al., 2008; Shenk, 2007; Dittmer, 2007). (This anticipated battle and its implications are further discussed in an upcoming section.) Hamas had previously survived off of donations from the Syrian, Iranian, and Qatari governments and is now headquartered in Damascus, though mainly operates in Palestine (Haughey, 2006). Today, Hamas has full governance of Gaza, though is recognized as a terror organization by both the United States and the European Court of Justice.

In 1993, to the dismay of Hamas, Israel Prime Minister Yitzhak Rabin and Chairman Yasser Arafat of the Palestine Liberation Organization signed a treaty between Israelis and Palestinians. Named "The Oslo Accords," the treaty effectively ended the First Intifada and brought peace between Israelis and Palestinians (Sabbah, 2015; Rydelnik, 2007). However, the peace was short-lived, and the Second

Intifada that followed the brief period of peace became even more devastating than the first one.

The Death of Oslo

Two years after the Oslo Accords were signed, Rabin was assassinated; a decade later, Arafat was poisoned – two killings that symbolize the failure of the treaty. Sen (2015) and Rydelnik (2007) argued that any attempt for reconciliation between Israelis and Palestinians in the current generation was slain when the Oslo Accords of 1993 failed. While the Oslo Accords achieved an end to the First Intifada (1987-1993) against Israel, this came to be only a short-term success. Due to the monumental effects of the Oslo Accords' failure, many resources have been spent analyzing why the deal seemed to crumble (Golan, 2015a).

In short, the Oslo Accords were a declaration of principles (not unlike the UN's Universal Declaration of Human Rights) that were intended to act as a peace treaty. It was a compromise signed by both the Israeli government and the Palestinian Authority in 1993, which outlined specific steps each nation was to take in order to achieve better peace. At the risk of oversimplifying a detailed and nuanced document that took two governing bodies nearly a half-year to create, the Oslo Accords outlined an agreement in which Israelis would concede Jericho, Gaza, and the West Bank to Palestinians in exchange for a concerted effort by Palestinians to stop terroristic efforts against Israelis. This included a promise from Palestine to recognize Israel as a sovereign nation (as was the UN's stance), denounce terrorism, prosecute Palestinian terrorists, and create a police force to enforce these tenets.

The Oslo Accords appeared to be a promising resolution to the longstanding Israeli-Palestinian Conflict. This was symbolized as much by a rare handshake between Israeli Prime Minister Yitzhak Rabin and Palestinian *de facto* leader Yasser Arafat. Unfortunately, the Oslo Accords were as fleeting as a simple handshake as the treaty quickly fell apart (Rydelnik, 2007). There are several reasons the Oslo Accords fell apart, and of course, depending on which side of the story one listens to, one will come to a different conclusion. That being said, there are some empirical points to consider regarding the failure of the treaty.

In the Oslo Accords, the Palestinian Authority promised to revise their Palestinian National Charter. At the time of agreement, the charter refused to recognize Israel as a state, and demanded the destruction of the nation. As part of the Oslo Accords, the charter would be revised to call for the systematic pushback against anti-Israel sentiment, including the eradication of hostile propaganda and active participation in fighting against Palestinian terror cells. This included a provision that the Palestinian Authority would arrest and prosecute those engaged in terrorism against Israel. The Oslo Accords also called for a limit on weapons and soldiers that would be harbored in Palestinian territory.

The Palestinian National Charter was never revised, and there is little evidence that the Palestinian Authority (PA) combatted anti-Israel sentiment (Rydelnik, 2007, p. 19). The PA continued endorsing elementary textbooks that denigrated Jews, with one 4th grade textbook stating, "Treachery and disloyalty are character traits of the Jews and one should be aware of them" (Kressel, 2007, p. 208). The U.S. State Department formally acknowledged that both Hamas and the PA continued to "publish and broadcast anti-Semitic incitement and call for the death of Jews" (Tobin, 2012, p. 4). The European Association of Geographers have noted that Palestinian maps issued by the PA omit the Green Line (i.e., the internationally recognized border between Israel and Palestine) and also omit the name "Israel" from appearing anywhere on the map, effectively implying that the PA did not recognize Israel to actually have control over any of the land (Medzini, 2012). And though the PA did occasionally arrest suspected terrorists, they often released them right away without a trial (Rydelnik, 2007). Further, the Oslo Accords set a limit of Palestinian soldiers at 30,000, but Palestine kept a consistent strength of 40,000 troops, along with an excess of weapons prohibited in the Oslo Accords (Rydelnik, 2007).

On the other end of the deal, Israel promised to give land to Palestine at certain deadlines, but those deadlines came and passed without land concession. The claim from Israel was that the

Palestinian Authority was charged with honoring their ends of the deal first (specifically, revising the Palestinian National Charter before land concession), and because that did not happen, Israel became hesitant to withdraw from any of their land. Israel *did* withdraw from their land, but it was slower than agreed upon, and strategically executed. For example, while Israel withdrew their troops from certain areas, approximately 740 Palestinian homes were demolished in other areas (Omeish & Omeish, 2006). These demolishes have not ceased, and figures from 2016 put the number of Palestinian homes that have been razed at 28,000 (Jhally, Alper, & Earp, 2016).

This had a twofold effect on Palestinians: Palestinians who believed in the effort to peace were disappointed by Israel's lack of concession and outright aggression, while Palestinians who had no stock or understanding of the peace treaty saw it as a sign of great weakness from Israel (i.e., that Israel would withdraw at all despite the Palestinian Authority not having to make any major changes). What once seemed like a step in the direction of peace became a lose-lose for the reconciliation process.

Just three years after the treaty was signed, one specific event occurred that symbolized the rapid deterioration of the peace treaty. In 1996, the Hasmonean Tunnel (near the Western Wall) was given an expansion to provide easier access for tourists exiting the Temple Mount. The expansion had been negotiated and agreed upon by the Palestinian Authority, but when Prime Minister Netanyahu opened the tunnel and trekked across the expansion, PA leader Arafat told people to protest Israel and said that it was a "big crime against our religion and holy places" (Rydelnik, 2007, p. 19). Israel expressed frustration that this was nothing more than anti-Israel propaganda, as the Palestinian Authority had been a part of approving the expansion in the first place.

At this point, the execution of the terms of the Oslo Accords was being slowed already, but it ultimately failed when Israel refused to concede land back to Palestine. Israelis argued that Palestinians had already violated the agreement, and that Israel therefore should not be expected to concede any of its land. Palestinians instead argued that the concession of land was a concrete promise by Israel, and that they were the ones not holding up their end of the bargain.

In May 2000, the death of the Oslo Accords received its exclamation point when Israelis entered Lebanon to fight Hezbollah, a Lebanese-based political party that is widely recognized as a terror cell by the western world and the Arab League (Gleis & Berti, 2012; Difference Between, 2017). Hezbollah was no stranger to the Arab-Israeli Conflict; the group had frequently launched offensives against Israel and often allied with Hamas and Palestinians since its inception in 1985. In retaliation to the violent outbreaks from Hezbollah against the Jews, Israelis invaded South Lebanon. After a quickly-agreed-upon peace agreement with the Lebanese government, Israel withdrew its troops. Hezbollah saw the withdrawal as a sign of Israeli weakness (as opposed to a path to peace), and claimed military victory. This victory cry incited more Palestinian terrorists, who appeared to be motivated by this victory over Israel. The *Crescent International*, a Muslim newspaper, reported of this incident:

> [Arafat] has been coming under increasing pressure since the liberation of south Lebanon, which had the effect of a match thrown into the tinderbox of accumulated Palestinian fury. Hezbollah's example has given Palestinians a powerful and attractive contrast, an example worthy of being emulated. In Lebanon, the Islamic resistance's unwavering determination succeeded in bringing about total liberation with no strings attached. (Osman, 2000)

Last Attempt at Peace

United States President Bill Clinton, hampered by the Monica Lewinsky affair and subsequent impeachment, was in need of a significant political victory in mid-2000 during the last leg of his tenure as president. Hoping that his legacy could be stamped by peace in the Middle East rather than his extramarital relationship with an intern, peace talks were convened in July 2000 at Camp David (Rydelnik, 2007). While Prime Minister of Israel, Ehud Barak, was motivated to engage in peace talks, he warned before the event that, if Camp David II (as it would become known) were to fail, then its failure would almost certainly lead to even greater violence after the event than before.

Prime Minister Barak's words became more harrowing as Camp David II failed and, less than three months later, full-fledged war broke out as Palestinians launched the Second Intifada that would last until 2005. Israel supporters claim that PA leader Arafat came to the Camp David Summit without any intention of actually agreeing to a peace deal (Rydelnik, 2007). This sentiment was echoed by President Clinton, who said of the meeting, "I think it is fair to say that at this moment in time, maybe because they had been preparing for it longer, maybe because they had thought through it more, that [Israeli Prime Minister Barak] moved forward more from his initial position than Chairman Arafat" (Clinton, 2000).

Meanwhile in Israel, Israeli President Ariel Sharon was under intense scrutiny for having entered al-Aqsa Mosque, the third-holiest site in Islam that sits right next to the Dome of the Rock. While Sharon initially had gotten permission from the Palestinian Authority to do so, PA leaders warned Sharon that it would likely be ill-received by Muslims. Unfazed, Sharon entered the mosque to make a clear statement that the Temple Mount is for everybody, not just Muslims. As warned, this act was not received well by Palestinians living in Jerusalem. These Palestinians began to hurl stones at Jews worshiping at the Western Wall, which prompted Israeli police to swiftly respond with tear gas and rubber bullets. Jews and Palestinians alike were injured in the incident, and the Second Intifada broke out in the days following Sharon's visit.

As the informal war intensified, Israel put together the Israel Defense Forces (IDF), which aimed to kill terrorists *in the act of carrying out terror*. Very quickly, the IDF became a force that attempted to *prevent* terror, which often resulted in both would-be-terrorists and innocent civilians being killed before any act was actually carried out. While Israel claimed self-defense, the NATO Rules of Engagement explicitly prohibited this exercise of force (as it allows too much power to individual countries in deciding who is deemed a terrorist).

The United States, the United Nations, the European Union, and Russia recognized the seriousness of this escalation of force, and developed a neutral deal in 2003 called the Road Map to Peace. The Quartet (as the US, UN, EU, and Russia would become known) intervened by deeming that Palestine would become a state immediately and get some land, but that the Palestinian government would need to be developed and would have a charge to stop the terrorism being carried out against Israel. Israel and Palestine agreed to this deal, and a ceasefire occurred. Despite this ceasefire, Palestinian terrorism continued, and the Palestinian Authority (which became the *de facto* government of this supposed sovereign state of Palestine) did not take any counter-measures to stop the attacks against Israel by terrorists.

Israel petitioned to the United States to lift the ceasefire, claiming their hands were tied and unable to defend themselves against the onslaught of attacks from Hamas, and that the Israeli-Palestinian Conflict could not be solved without the full cooperation of Hamas anyway (Zuhur et al., 2008). United States President Bush agreed to lift the ban, and Israel was allowed to again retaliate against Hamas. The fighting intensified, Mahmoud Abbas resigned as Prime Minister of Palestine, and the Road Map to Peace crumbled. Three years later in 2006, the Second Lebanon War broke out. Though the formal war technically ended in the same year it started, at the time of this publication, fighting has not stopped.

Contemporary Violations of International Law and Human Rights

Anna Baltzer, a Jewish-American who spent five months in the West Bank, could not use her fidelity to the Jewish ethnicity to justify what she saw happening to Palestinians during her stay. Baltzer has emphasized the stark contrast in the living conditions between the Israelis and Palestinians. For instance, Baltzer explains that Israelis and Palestinians live in segregation, even to the point where some highways are only to be used by Israelis while others can only be used by Palestinians. Naturally, the Palestinian roads are decrepit and nearly impassable, while Israeli roads are well-paved and smooth (Films for Action, 2009). Many de-segregated roads have curfews for Palestinians only – even Americans, Egyptians, Lebanese, and Syrians are not held to this curfew like Palestinians are. There are numerous checkpoints on roads that Palestinians are allowed to use, so what might be a 30- or 40- minute drive for an Israeli would amount to several hours because of the traffic-jammed checkpoints for Palestinians. This makes it hard for Palestinians to hold steady jobs near Jerusalem because going to work could take a Palestinian anywhere between 30 minutes and three hours on any given day.

Baltzer also recounts a Palestinian woman who had gone into labor shortly after midnight (i.e., during the dusk-to-dawn curfew imposed on Palestinians), and the Israelis would not let her pass through, even to just get to a hospital to safely deliver her twin babies. The woman spent the night in labor in her car, unable to pass the checkpoint. When the curfew was lifted at 7am, she was allowed to pass through and get to the hospital, but the hospital was not able to save either of the twins as they had gone without post-natal care for too many hours (Films for Action, 2009). The right to movement is specifically outlined in the Universal Declaration of Human Rights, and these checkpoints that prevent access to healthcare and schools are in direct opposition to international law (Omeish & Omeish, 2006).

Perhaps the most egregious form of oppression – one that is decried around the world – is the Israeli occupation of Palestinian settlements (Films for Action, 2009; Jhally, Alper, & Earp, 2016). Despite it being a violation of international law, Israelis have set up camps in Palestinian territory (Robinson, 1997). The Israeli government has officially denied being responsible for these illegal settlements, but an overwhelming amount of evidence has indicated that the Israeli government has commissioned many of these settlements (Films for Action, 2009). At times, the Israeli government has offered financial compensation to Israelis willing to move into these camps, which is especially burdensome on Palestinians as this often results in poor, uneducated, and pernicious Israelis being the ones who move into these settlements. It is, therefore, not shocking that Israelis are viewed as an oppressive enemy to Palestinians, and "Palestinian martyrs are celebrated, honored, and publicized on mural and posters" for their opposition to the state of Israel (Piven, 2017, p. 89).

Prognosis

The issues here are so complicated that I cannot even provide a number of how many Jews and Arabs have been victims of the conflict because as soon as I do, I am accused of being biased for using a number that does not fit in with one of the two main narratives. The Jewish and Palestinian narratives are that divided. Conflict resolution and reconciliation efforts have been made from many different (and sometimes creative) angles, yet no resolution has been able to sustain long-term peace. Even the most promising theoretical resolutions have not been sustainable outside of a sterile laboratory environment (Jones, 2016). Ceasefire has been a constant endgame but also a constant failure: truly, 100% of ceasefire attempts have failed in Israel's history (Rydelnik, 2007).

One of the contributing factors to these failed attempts is that it is difficult to measure which side is truly to blame when a ceasefire fails. In the Israeli-Palestinian Conflict, it is clear that both sides see themselves as the victims of the conflict (as opposed to the perpetrators). In Israelis' minds, most of their violence is justified as it is an act of retaliation (as opposed to malevolence) to Palestinian violence. Haushofer, Biletzki, and Kanwisher (2010) admit that past research does show that Israeli violence is largely retaliatory while Palestinian violence is often instigative, however, they also argue that statistics do not tell the whole story. Consider this: 95% of the West Bank is comprised of Palestinians who have claimed the land through peace treaties and deals over the decades (Omeish & Omeish, 2006). At first glance, this statistic seems like an admirable compromise by Israelis. However, the remaining Israelis that make up the final 5% are the ones in control: the military, the government, the police. Omeish and Omeish compare this arrangement to that of a prison, where 95% of the prison is comprised of prisoners, while the guards and warden make up the final 5%. Despite the fact that the prisoners outnumber the authority, they are not actually free.

Likewise, it is said that Israel relinquished control of Gaza in 2005, but Yousef Munayyer of the US Campaign to End the Israeli Occupation says this idea is "100% bogus" because even though Israel did reduce physical bodies in Gaza, they simultaneously increased control by disallowing vehicle and air movement (Jhally, Alper, & Earp, 2016). Phyllis Bennis of the Institute for Policy Studies states that despite the Israeli narrative that they have relinquished Gaza, "Gaza remains occupied. Gaza has no control over its coast, over its waters, over its harbor, over its airspace, over the land or its borders, over its people. Who can come and go is totally at the Israeli discretion" (Jhally, Alper, & Earp, 2016). It is sovereignty – not just an arbitrary proportion of land – that Palestinians seek.

Haushofer et al. (2010) conducted a study to further illustrate the bias in statistics reported about the Israeli-Palestinian Conflict. Using econometrics, the researchers measured the amount of proclaimed self-defense to assess how much of the violence in the conflict was retaliatory rather than instigative. The researchers found their data aligning with previous research in that Israeli violence often increases after Palestinian violence, however, the researchers differed from previous research in arguing that – like Israeli violence – most Palestinian violence was also retaliatory. The researchers argue that the discrepancy is twofold: first, many researchers refuse to admit their cognitive biases to the extent to which each side is simply retaliating (as opposed to instigating). Secondly and more importantly, most of the previous research has used limited datasets that have only measured lethal violence rather than nonlethal violence. For instance, it is illegal for Israel Defense Forces (IDF) to shoot women or children with rubber-coated metal bullets; it is illegal for IDF to shoot *anyone* with these rubber-bullets closer than 50 meters; and it is illegal for IDF to shoot someone with these rubber-bullets unless the recipient of the bullet is a threat to life or limb. Yet, these rubber-bullets have been used to cripple children as close as five meters away in retaliation to the child cursing at a soldier (Jhally, Alper, & Earp, 2016). In another situation, a rubber-bullet hit a Palestinian's car and it shattered the car window, blinding a young girl who was a passenger in the vehicle; Jhally, Alper, and Earp (2016) conjecture that it was highly unlikely this would ever be reported by IDF. Haushofer et al. (2010) argue that if more data was collected on the extent to which Israelis nonlethally provoke Palestinians, there would be a greater balance of retaliatory impetus (and thus less data that Palestinians are instigators).

Of course, from a historical perspective, placing blame does little to ultimately promote peace and, in fact, often works for the opposite endgame. Brueggemann (2015) argued that, regardless of religious or ethnic affiliation, it must be recognized that both Israelis and Palestinians have contributed to the unnecessary and extreme violence in the conflict. This stance can perhaps be succinctly illustrated by considering the current leadership in Israel and Palestine: the current President of the Palestinian Liberation Organization, Mahmoud Abbas, is chairman of the al-Fatah movement, which was birthed in the 1950s out of a goal to destroy Israel; meanwhile, the current Israeli Prime Minister, Benjamin Netanyahu, is chairman of the Likud-National Liberal Movement, whose charter insists that Israelis have the right to settle on Palestinian land (Jhally, Alper, & Earp, 2016).

As a result, every proposed treaty between Israelis and Palestinians has been rejected by one or both sides, and often these proposals did not offer immediate tangible benefits for either side. Further, all of the peace proposals requested the Palestinians to give up their one bargaining chip (i.e., violence) while Israel would get to keep hers (i.e., land). Palestinians see these proposals as attempts to return to the way it has always been, leaving the future of Israel hard to determine.

Of course, the prognosis of the fighting between Jews and Palestinians varies depending on who is discussing it. However, Sabella (2019), Rydelnik (2007), and Brueggemann (2015) are part of the majority of scholars who believe that the two-state solution is an impossible solution, as it requires one side to concede and, in essence, give up the claim to Jerusalem. This compromise is a fanciful wish, partially due to the fact that each two-state solution has been viewed as largely benefitting Israel, serving as a means for the nation to buy time as owners of the land. Israeli historian Illan Pappe of Haifa University warns:

> Anybody outside of Israel who supports a two-state solution has to be very careful, because what they mean in "two-state solution" is 90% of historical Palestine will be Israel, and the

rest 10% will have two huge prison camps – one in the Gaza Strip and one in the West Bank. (Omeish & Omeish, 2006)

Walter Brueggemann offers a unique take on the Israeli-Palestinian Conflict due to his background as being a scholar of the Hebrew Bible while simultaneously being a scholar of the Israeli-Palestinian Conflict. Brueggemann (2015) has specifically homed in on the problem of ideologies, displaying repugnance for any absolutist stance, which he claims are impractical for real-world situations. Brueggemann makes the case that religious ideologies have dominated the Israeli-Palestinian Conflict, and that the United States is just as guilty as anyone for propagating one-sided ideologies. Brueggemann makes the biblical case that, even if the Jews have been "chosen" by God as the rightful heirs of Israel (which he *does* believe to be true), it does not mean that they are above accountability: there are a plethora of instances in the Bible in which God revokes the land He gave to Israel. Furthermore, Brueggemann (2015) argued that the ancient Israelites who were given these promises by God are essentially a different people than the Israelites of today, who have since become a military superpower – though some Jews, Christians, and even Arabs would vehemently disagree with this last supposition. Ultimately, Brueggemann has speculated that perhaps the best outcome is a one-state solution in which the Jews are given the entire state of Israel, with the condition that these Jews must ensure the human rights of Palestinians who reside as citizens. Of course, this solution is overly idealistic as similar "compromises" have been surmised.

Like Brueggemann, Bar-Tal and Halperin (2014) highlighted the need for more honest assessments of the Israeli-Palestinian Conflict and agree that the two-state solution will always be set up to fail for four reasons. First, there is no breaking through the fact that both Israelis and Palestinians believe they have the primary right to own the land. Secondly, both Israelis and Palestinians see themselves as victims, and as such, will not rest until justice is served in their eyes. Thirdly, both sides have a fear that any compromise will result in their eventual extermination, thus defeating the purpose of any negotiations. Finally, the storied history between the two sides and their animosity towards one another will forever undermine peace negotiations. It is not unlike a legal case in which two parties are meeting with a mediator, but have no intent on settling the case outside of court: if Israel and Palestine have a strong belief that the land should be theirs and theirs alone, then what value would it be to them to negotiate a compromise that feels like justice has fallen short?

Elman (2016) does not explicitly evaluate a two-state solution, though she does agree that land is the main issue at stake in this conflict. Elman contends that compromise is possible, but only if both sides are willing to make considerable concessions. However, bearing in mind again the position taken by Cole and Hatano (2010) that the land of Israel is not just soil but a meaningful religious symbol that regulates psychological processes, the prospect of peace takes a cynical turn: the issue is a land dispute, but even larger than that, it is a religious dispute.

The resolution between Israelis and Palestinians quickly tapered following the Oslo Accords, but since the open-ended "conclusion" of the Second Intifada, the conflict has remained at a lull with only occasional headlines across the years (Golan, 2015a; Isaac, 2017). However, in the 70 years between 1948 and 2018, Israel's population increased by a whopping eight million people (see Table 2). As the population in Israel and Palestine continues to climb, so will the violent incidents. The relatively-stable relationship between Israelis and Palestinians in recent years is believed to be a false peace, and history assures that this false peace will manifest its true nature in the coming years (Haushofer et al., 2010; Sabella, 2019; Rydelnik, 2007; Brueggemann, 2015; Nets-Zehngut, 2014). Herein lies the state of the Israeli-Palestinian Conflict today: a stalemate that claims the lives of more Jews and more Arabs for each passing day the issue remains gridlocked.

TABLE 2: Israel population by year (Katz & Lavee, 2004; World Bank, 2018)

Year	Population	Reason for Increase	Notes
1915	689,275		Considered Ottoman Palestine
1948	873,000	Holocaust survivors (and their descendants) flock to Israel	Some Arabs claim Holocaust never happened, and was a Jewish strategy to capitalize on Palestinian land
2004	6,500,000	USSR dissolution of 1991 and Ethiopian sociopolitical strife of 1991 result in former Soviet residents and Ethiopian Jews (or Beta Israelis) fleeing to Israel	There is internal debate within the Jewish community as to whether Ethiopian immigrants who claim Jewish roots are actually Jewish
2018	8,712,000	Anti-Semitism rises in some European countries, prompting more immigration from Anglo-Jews; Birth rate exponentially increases in Israel	Israel population is expected to continue to surge, which will result in more Israelis creating settlements in Palestinian territory, exacerbating the conflict

Problem Statement

Since its most recent inception as a sovereign state in 1948, Israel has been at war (Cole & Hatano, 2010). While most recognize their right to exist as a state, others have refused their claims of independence and dispute their borders (Jhally, Alper, & Earp, 2016; Shenk, 2007; Rydelnik, 2007). In 1993, a landmark peacemaking event occurred, in which the Palestinian Authority (PA) signed a peace treaty with the Israeli government, and a Declaration of Principles was agreed upon in 1993. The stakes were high, and Israeli Prime Minister Ehud Barak said that if the Oslo Accords failed, then violence would increase and peace might never be possible through compromise.

Today, "the Oslo Accords are dead, as are multitudes of Israelis and Palestinians" (Rydelnik, 2007, p. 18). As Prime Minister Barak predicted, violence surged after the failure of the Oslo Accords, and war erupted in 2000. It has thus been proposed that compromise may never work as a means to resolve the Israeli-Palestinian conflict, and instead, efforts should be focused on reconciliation (Friedman, 2016; Sabbah, 2015). The Israeli-Palestinian conflict is not isolated as it has prompted global tension. There is a cycle in which war-like mindsets are being passed down from generation to generation, and reconciliation and forbearance may be necessary to mitigate the conflict instead. Peacemakers' human efforts on compromise will never work; it is time to consider if reconciliation is possible without compromise. The first step of reconciliation is to understand the damage (i.e., the trauma) that has been done.

Unfortunately, posttraumatic stress disorder (PTSD) is the main framework still used to understand trauma in the Middle East (Wamser-Nanney & Vandenberg, 2013; Tennant, 2004; Vered & Bar-Tal, 2014; Dickstein et al., 2011). However, the clinical diagnosis of posttraumatic stress disorder (PTSD) was first developed in the DSM-III of 1980 because of America's need to understand the psychological trauma that Vietnam War veterans were displaying (Aupperle, 2018). Of the 135 studies that shaped the DSM diagnosis of PTSD, *two-thirds* of those studies were conducted in the United States and were not culturally validated beyond those borders (De Girolamo & McFarlane, 1996).

It is a considerable problem that a concept (i.e., PTSD) that has largely been only understood in western contexts is being applied in non-western contexts. It is possible – if not likely – that a phenomenon separate from PTSD is manifesting in non-western situations. If the field continues to insist on using PTSD as the baseline framework for trauma in these contexts, then we might never understand trauma in the non-western world. Important questions will remain unanswered: "What causes trauma?" "How does it manifest in protracted social conflicts?" "Is western trauma different from a non-western setting?" There are currently no comprehensive studies in western psychology that speak clearly enough about how trauma is translated or responded to in the Middle East.

A further nuance to this problem is that religion plays an important role in the identities of Israelis and Palestinians (Cole & Hatano, 2010; Wyshak, 2016; Shenk, 2007). This means that there exists a possibility that Middle Eastern trauma is interlinked also with sufferers' religious identities. Further, both Judaism and Islam have an overlapping eschatological prophecy found in both of their religious texts that speaks to how they should respond to the trauma when this unfulfilled prophecy comes to pass. Yet, I have yet to find a single scholarly article on this topic from a psychological perspective. It seems curious that a topic of this magnitude has yet to be given attention in the literature.

Purpose of the Study

The broad purpose of this study was to examine how the perpetual state of war in Israel and the religious beliefs of Jews and Muslims affect the psychological processing of the region's inhabitants. Practically speaking, ten Israelis and seven Palestinians who have experienced both direct and indirect trauma were interviewed to better understand the manifestation of their traumatic symptoms and the meaning-making process used to cope with those symptoms. The sample included both those who had engaged in combat and those who had not. The supposition was that regardless of whether or not they endured direct combat, a complex trauma was passed down to them; that is, even if an individual had never experienced direct fighting in the Israeli-Palestinian Conflict, they still remained in a state of hypervigilance that is often associated with trauma. Ultimately, the purpose of this study was to use a qualitative phenomenological methodology to explore how active participants of the Israeli-Palestinian conflict have passed down any traumatic symptoms to younger generations who have not had any direct role in the conflict. My intent in undertaking this study was to provide the reader with a concise history of the Israeli-Palestinian Conflict and to provide a broader understanding of the concept of trauma in Israel and Palestine, to include its religious and eschatological influences.

Research Questions and Hypotheses

Research Question 1: How does Transgenerational Trauma Transmission (TTT) manifest in Israeli and Palestinian young adults?

Research Question 2: How does religious identity affect the lenses of Israelis and Palestinians in conflict?

Theoretical Framework

Culture is simultaneously tangible and intangible: for every artifact containing culture, there is also an intangible symbol ingratiated into culture as well (Berry et al., 2011). Culture is therefore both internal and external and should be treated as such. In the Israeli-Palestinian Conflict, culture is embedded in both the concrete and abstract. For example, both Muslims and Jews adorn head coverings that are visually apparent, but many times, these head coverings have religious meaning as well that cannot be seen. Geertz (1973) argued that culture is not a formulaic or objective phenomenon but something that is subjective. Geertz described culture as a "historically transmitted pattern of meanings embodied in symbols" (p. 89), and within the Israeli-Palestinian Conflict specifically, we see this to be true with the actual land of Israel, which constitutes itself as a symbol that Jews and Arabs have deemed it worth dying over.

Van de Vijver et al. (2011) argued that a theoretical framework is in place to serve two purposes: to categorize studies into sub-categories (as characterized by categories that share theory and method) and to state explicitly the guidelines for future research. The Israeli-Palestinian Conflict is perhaps the most complicated conflict in modern history, and as such, it requires a distinctly cultural relativist psychological perspective, keeping in mind that the cultural relativist perspective relies on qualitative research and regards cultural contexts to be of paramount significance (Van de Vijver et al., 2011). The complexity of the conflict is a direct result of culture (including religious and political culture), and this is why a qualitative framework is favored over quantitative research. The relativist approach allows for a context-free examination of psychological functioning, and it cannot be cross-culturally studied as there are no other conflicts that are quite like the Israeli-Palestinian Conflict (Van de Vijver et al., 2011).

This study was driven by three specific theories: recognition theory, a construct universalist/relativistic hybrid theory, and, as will be discussed first, postmemory. Hirsch (1997) coined the term "postmemory," which she described as harsh memories that come after the traumatic memory, or literally, the "memory after the memory." The trauma, then, is not an actual event, but rather the passed down re-telling and/or memory of the event. Often, the details in that specific memory are inaccurate: an individual's overall narrative of a traumatic memory is often intact, but incorrect details plague the memory (Loftus, 2007). Over time, these false memories (or at least partially-incorrect memories) become as strong as the accurate components of the memory (Zhu et al., 2012).

Hirsch (1997) described a second generation of Holocaust survivors (i.e., children of Holocaust survivors) who were so influenced by their parents' tragedy that it is almost as if the second generation personally lived through the trauma. Despite having been born long after the Holocaust ended, these children inherited the tragedy (and subsequent trauma-related symptoms) into their own biography. The concept of intergenerational trauma is similar to complex trauma in that trauma-related symptoms may be seen in individuals who have not directly dealt with trauma, but there may exist a difference in the manifestation of the symptoms from individual to individual (Wamser-Nanney & Vandenberg, 2013). As such, intergenerational trauma has played a massive role in the legacy of the Israeli-Palestinian Conflict; this is not a conflict that spans a single generation but a vendetta that has been passed down from ancient ancestors to Israelis and Palestinians today (Brueggemann, 2015).

International psychology is considered to be a subset of psychology that seeks to conduct research in capacities that western research has missed or ignored altogether due to its biases (Berry et al., 2011). The term itself is an umbrella term for several culturally-related psychologies, most specifically cultural, cross-cultural, and indigenous psychology. Two of the fourfold conceptual theoretical frameworks as described by Fontaine (2011) have most relevance here: the relativistic perspective (or relativism) and construct universalism.

With the relativistic perspective, cultural comparison is not advantageous as each individual culture is self-producing and cannot be compared any better than one can compare apples and oranges, as it were (Fontaine, 2011). The premise of this concept is that psychological processes are affected solely by the culture (as opposed to innate traits), and are therefore completely culturally construed. This perspective contends that every individual has the innate ability to adapt into the culture they were born into, but that once they mature, they will never be able to seamlessly adapt into a different culture. In terms of international psychology, the indigenous psychological approach is most relativistic in nature as it investigates many constructs for which there is no western equivalent (Berry et al., 2011).

Fontaine (2011) presents the applied example of the Ilongot tribe in the Philippines, who have a particular emotion known as "liget." Unfortunately, there is no western equivalent to this concept, and therefore, it would be impossible to compare this concept. Another example of this is found in the Shurpu, the Babylonian medical text from the 17th century: the Babylonians refer to a phenomenon known as "mamit," which refers to a specific compulsion in which Babylonians felt compelled to touch spilled blood on animals or people that had been slain (Reynolds & Wilson, 2012). There has been an attempt to give this concept a western application, and it has often been roughly translated as meaning "oath," and thought of as a compulsion that is only seen in obsessive-compulsive disorder (Geist, 2016). However, the reality is that this concept is unique to the culture it was found in and there is no perfect equivalent in other cultures.

Similarly, the concept of trauma in Israel is unlike the same concept as seen in western psychology, which will be described later.

Fontaine (2011) also presents the construct universalist perspective, which contends that innate traits do, indeed, exist, but that it is *culture* that truly molds a person's psychological processes. Quantitative analysis can be used in this approach, but its use must be limited to innate traits. In general, quantitative analysis is not overly useful with this concept. Cultural psychology can be described as falling under either relativism or construct universalism, as it states the behavior and culture are inseparable, and while it does not deny that facets of universalism exist, it argues that it is not worth focusing on in comparison to the effect that culture has (Berry et al., 2011).

An applied example of this concept as provided by Fontaine (2011) is the concept of *greeting*. In Japan, individuals greet one another by bowing to each other. In the United States, individuals shake hands. These acts are obviously two different manifestations, but they are represented by the same concept of greeting. Another example of this would be *social status*: in the United States, social status is often gauged by the material possessions or power that a person has, but in other cultures, a person's status may increase with the number of relationships they have or by the amount of wisdom they are deemed to have.

Achieving a cognizance of relativism and construct universalism is helpful to both the researcher and potentially the reader in that it amplifies the idea that the Middle East has achieved its own culture and concepts apart from the western world. In terms of this study, as consideration is given to western psychological concepts that have firm backing – namely, trauma – it will also be necessary to accept that these concepts may have been mistranslated in other cultures. Practically speaking, the definitions of PTSD in both the American Psychiatric Association's 5th edition of the Diagnostic and Statistical Manual of Mental Disorders (DSM 5) and the World Health Organization's 10th edition of the International Classification of Diseases (ICD-10) may not parallel the reality of trauma in Israel and Palestine (Wamser-Nanney & Vandenberg, 2013; Tennant, 2004; Fontaine, 2011).

Maxwell (2004) emphasizes the importance of selectively choosing aspects of theories to create one's own research paradigm. Specifically, Maxwell encourages researchers to consider their own experiential knowledge, existing theory and research, pilot and exploratory research, and thought experiments when creating such a paradigm. Sinclair (2009) described his paradigm/framework as a travel itinerary, the idea being that travelers seek others' advice before traveling to a country they have never been. This itinerary helps travelers to know what to expect and what pitfalls to avoid, and a framework is exactly that: a way to put a basic idea into the context of an already-researched paradigm.

In this way, when considering Hirsch's concept of postmemory, along with the muddied religious history of the Israeli-Palestinian Conflict, my framework naturally gravitates towards a traditional qualitative design with an exploratory focus. From Fontaine's fourfold conceptual framework, a relativistic and construct universalistic perspective was taken. Rydelnik and Brueggemann both describe the phenomenon in which anybody living near Israel is unfairly but automatically a part of the Israeli-Palestinian Conflict, resulting in phenomena that are similar to Hirsch's postmemory (1997).

The methodological approach of the study was driven by recognition theory, which aims to bring awareness to the fact that every conflict can be seen from different vantages (Turney, 2012). Honneth (1995) argued that social conflicts can generally be characterized as a struggle to get one's opponent to recognize his/her view, so he developed recognition theory as the idea that an acknowledgement of an opponent's viewpoint results in strong conflict resolution. Friedman (2016) argued that recognition theory would likely work in helping to settle the Israeli-Palestinian Conflict and that without an acknowledgement that both Israelis and Palestinians alike have suffered from the conflict, resolution will never be possible.

Admittedly, the goal of this study was not to achieve resolution or reconciliation. That being said, Honneth (1995) introduced recognition theory as a tool to help infants develop a greater awareness of the world they cannot see. While conflict resolution is a positive byproduct of the theory, the aim is to help individuals gain a greater sense of their relationship with the world as "it is through the relational experience of recognition – recognizing and being recognized by the other – that the infant learns to understand him- or herself" (Turney, 2012, p. 151). After all, the aim of any intervention or research design should also serve the community that is being given the intervention or participating in the research (Miller & Rasco, 2004). As such, I used recognition theory and the participatory action model as designed by Hugman, Pittaway, and Bartolomei (2011) in order to ensure participants felt a sense of belonging to the research and to maintain the integrity of this project as a community-focused endeavor in which the participants truly care about the end result. The participatory action model and recognition theory's roles in this study are expounded upon in Chapter 3.

Scope and Delimitations

Ellis and Levy (2009) described the scope as the zeroed-in topic of a study. In this instance, the Israeli-Palestinian Conflict is a storied topic, so having a specific scope is crucial. The research was characterized by the following three aspects that make up the scope: 1) the Israeli-Palestinian Conflict as it is understood from the context of Israeli gaining state sovereignty in 1948 (i.e., conflict events before 1948 were not analyzed, with the exception of religious texts); 2) the religious and eschatological connotations of the history of the Israeli-Palestinian Conflict, including the Gog and Magog battle recognized by all three Abrahamic religions; and 3) trauma as defined by modern western terminology (i.e., ICD-10 and/or DSM 5) versus how trauma is operationalized in Middle Eastern culture.

Ellis and Levy (2009) also note that the delimitations of a study are important as they act as the intentional buffers that have been put in place to achieve to scope. The four delimitations of this study are as follows: 1) participants are limited to those who live, or have recently lived (i.e., since 2005), in Israeli or Palestinian territory; 2) while the history of the conflict needs to be explored, the purpose of this research is not to see who is "right or wrong" in the conflict; 3) personal narratives are necessary to appreciate participants' experiences on a qualitative level, but the initial direction of these interviews was informed by evidence-based data; and 4) no audio or visual recording devices were used during data collection in an effort to minimize the Hawthorne Effect and to maximize the participants' comfort level with the researcher.

Definition of Key Terms

Religion

Ferré (1970) argued that the word "religion" has many different functions – most usually as a vehicle for technical, moralistic, or ethnic classification. In simpler terms, when I say "religion," I likely have a different understanding of the word's meaning than another individual. Further, if I am in a synagogue and use the word "Jewish," this likely will have a different connotation than if I were in an Israeli courthouse and used the same word. For this reason and for the purpose of this study, when I speak of religion, I speak of a person's specific set of hortatory, foundational beliefs that are generally agreed upon by others claiming to be of the same religion.

Jews, Muslims, and Christians

Those of the Jewish religion are those who contemplate the Torah or the entire Tanakh, and believe Jacob is the anointed offspring of Isaac (Molloy, 2013). Those of the Muslim religion are those who abide by the Qur'an and believe Ishmael to be the anointed offspring of Isaac. Those of the Christian religion are those who adhere to the Christian Holy Bible as authoritative, and believe Jesus (or Yeshua) of Nazareth to be the first incarnation of the peaceful Jewish Messiah (or Christ), and that Jesus (or Yeshua) will have a second incarnation as the conquering Jewish Messiah.

Jewish vs Israeli

This gets difficult as the Jewish ethnicity is often synonymous with the Jewish religion. In this study, I will attempt to differentiate between those who adhere to Judaism as a religion ("Jewish") and those who are simply of Jewish descent. The important takeaway here is that a person who is referred to be of "Jewish descent" is not

38

automatically assumed to be Jewish, though anyone referred to as a Muslim is understood in the religious context of this word.

Palestinian Authority

More specific to this study, the Palestinian Authority (PA) needs to be operationalized. When the PA is being referenced, it is referring to the governing body of Palestine that was created in the 1990s in response to the Oslo Accords (Robinson, 1997; Rydelnik, 2007). Some associate the PA with terrorism because Yasser Arafat was elected as its first president in 1996. In this study, when the PA is referenced, it is simply referring to the governing body of Palestine and not with its alleged associations with terrorism.

Terrorism

Another issue of contention is the word "terrorism." For the purposes of this study, the phrases "terrorism," "terror attacks," and other terror-related maxim will only be referred to as such if at least one government (i.e., Israeli government or Palestinian Authority) has formally identified the incident or tactic as having been terroristic in nature. The reason that it is important to refer to a labeled terrorist attack as such – regardless of the potential opposition to the label – is because this study is hoping to offer a sense of validation to the ethnic narratives of the individual participants within the study. Simply put, if an ethnic group regards an event as being an instance of terrorism, then it must be understood as such in order to achieve a grasp of their overarching narrative.

PTSD vs Trauma

There is also need for an operational definition of trauma. Haj (2015) emphasized that the concept of PTSD in the United States is different than what is typically thought of as trauma in the Middle East. Abusoboh (2016), a native Palestinian who has gone on to study the effects of trauma in higher education, observes that PTSD is simply not applicable in Palestine. Abusoboh argues that using PTSD diagnoses and PTSD treatment plans ignores the ethnocultural factors of trauma from viewpoints outside of the western world. She suggests that more qualitative studies that eschew the assumptions of the western notion of PTSD will be needed if the Palestinian notion of trauma is to be understood and ultimately addressed by mental health professionals. For these reasons, PTSD will not be interchangeable with trauma: PTSD will remain as it is understood by the DSM 5 and ICD-10, whereas trauma refers to any significant event in which an individual was in danger of losing their life and had perceptible or imperceptible negative consequences that occurred during the time of the traumatic event (Wamser-Nanney & Vandenberg, 2013; Tennant, 2004). The operationalization of the phenomenon that this research is intending to focus on, Transgenerational Trauma Transmission (TTT), will be presented in the following chapter as the definition can be best understood in the context of the literature review that follows.

A Note on the Refugee Status of the Participants

It is important to acknowledge – not only as a baseline understanding of the levels of trauma experienced by participants, but also as a design consideration and ethical assurance – that this study's entire sample had probably suffered from trauma on some level. According to Katz and Lavee (2004), "the percentage of Israeli families who have suffered injury or loss, or who have close relatives or personal friends who have experienced this suffering, approaches 100%" (p. 495). The sensitivity to the topic cannot be overstated.

Another confounding factor is the financial differences between Israelis and Palestinians. To put this into context, consider a study conducted by Mock et al. (2012) that sought to better understand the gap between current trauma care and ideal trauma care in financially unstable countries. To do so, Mock et al. looked at data for fatality rates of injured people in Seattle, USA (high income), Monterrey, Mexico (middle income), and Kumasi, Ghana (low income) and assessed the mortality rate for similar injuries across the three samples. The researchers found that nearly 2,000,000 lives could be saved if low-income and middle-income areas had the same resources and care available as in high income areas. Granted, a limitation of this study is that reporting accuracy may also be variable between Seattle, Monterrey, and Kumasi, which would affect the end conclusions.

Israel proper is considered a high-income area (Cole & Hatano, 2010), which is astonishing when one considers that the rest of the Middle East generally falls into the mid- to low-income ranges. Palestinians – even those who live in Israel – tend to fall into the lower end of the economic stability scales. The fact that many Israelis have financial stability (while many Palestinians do not) indicates that Israelis are prepositioned to also have better health care opportunities than Palestinians. For the purposes of this research, it should be kept in mind that Palestinians may have had fewer resources than their Israeli counterparts in processing their trauma in a formal mental health setting.

Further, there are even significant differences that distinguish one Israeli community from another. Stein et al. (2013) studied two different communities in Israel. Though both were Israeli communities, their cultural circumstances could not have been more different: those in the Sderot community have a history of poverty and marginalization, and could be compared to what is known as a "project community" in the United States. Stein et al. also looked at Israelis in the Otef Aza community. The Otef Aza community was built to be a *kibbutz*, which is essentially the Israeli take on trying to achieve a utopian society where the community is cohesive and self-sufficient and, therefore, often well-resourced. Stein et al. sampled 298 residents of Sderot and 152 residents in Otef Aza ($N = 450$). What the researchers found was that terrorism seemed to affect the residents of Sderot much more deeply than the residents of Otef Aza. Specifically, those residents of Sderot were much more likely to be diagnosed with PTSD, depression, and other anxiety disorders, despite not having significantly different exposure to trauma than those in Otef Aza.

There were many reasons why Sderot residents were more likely to be affected by trauma. First, Sderot reported significantly higher property loss (and loss of life) during trauma situations. This indicates that those in poorer communities are not as equipped to handle a crisis like a rocket attack. Secondly, those in Sderot were much more likely to have been divorced, widowed, or separated and therefore much less likely to have the same level of the support networks as in Otef Aza. Finally, those in Sderot were less likely to have resources to help them cope after an attack, whereas services like counseling were available to those in Otef Aza.

There is much difference between the Otef Aza and Sderot communities – both of which might simply be clumped together as "Israelis" in other studies. If this delta exists across Israeli communities, then it seems obvious that this situation could be present in Palestinian communities, too. For instance, a researcher is likely going to get a much different story if he/she only interviews the Palestinians who are allowed to live in Jerusalem. A study that fails to gain access into Palestinian camps is likely to be negatively impacted by having only obtained the "privileged" Palestinian narrative. Based on Stein et al. (2013), such a situation is especially problematic: not only would a significant chunk of the narrative be missing, but the study would probably be presented as having included "the Palestinian narrative" when, in reality, a large sample of Palestinians had not even been able to contribute to the study.

Neither Israelis nor modern-day settled Palestinians are considered to have refugee status by the United Nations, nor is either group protected as a vulnerable population by the United States government (Al Husseini, Bocco, Brunner, & Bühler, 2007). The UN does recognize some Palestinians as having refugee status, but this is limited to those Palestinians who were part of the original exile between 1946 and 1948 (UNRWA, 2017). Despite this non-refugee status, it is wise to approach this population as if they were, for both Israelis and Palestinians share many characteristics of refugees and the argument has been made that Israel-dwelling Palestinians are, in fact, still refugees today (Al Husseini et al., 2007).

Miller and Rasco (2004) seem to agree as they similarly argue that refugee situations exist whenever a people's resources do not meet their needs. This formula seems to hold true for most international rescue efforts, whose focus tends to be increasing resources to help mitigate the problems faced by refugees. Psychological problems are a reflection of the inaccessibility of adaptive resources within the specific setting that people live and breathe in every day. As a result of this tension, relief efforts and interventions are geared to do one of three actions: mitigate these problems within the present ecological settings, create ecological settings that are better suited for the people's needs, or empower and enhance the people's capacity to adapt effectively to their present environment.

Further, interventions that only focus on issues that the targeted community does not believe to be problems are ineffective (Miller & Rasco, 2004). Intervention efforts need to reflect the needs as understood by the community. Prevention is preferred over treatment because preventative interventions are more effective in the long-term, generally less expensive, and often more humane than implementing interventions only when problems arise.

Specific to the Israeli-Palestinian Conflict, the heart of the issue is about land (Sabbah, 2015), which is often one of the primary problems within a refugee crisis. Even if not officially labeled by the UN as such, those who claim they do not have their rightful land (i.e., namely Palestinians) often see themselves as refugees. Confounding this element is the fact that much of the crux of the issue is often boiled down to a misunderstanding of each other's values and belief systems, particularly in regards to religious disagreement (and religious heirs of land) between Muslims and Jews.

When researchers are working with populations who fit this type of criterion, the systems that are already in place should be used rather than trying to invent completely new interventions (Miller & Rasco, 2004). In order to truly help any refugee population with their psychological needs, it is necessary to understand the needs in the context of the refugees themselves. This requires an understanding of the refugees' personal belief system and values as they are reported, rather than from any preconceived notions. This helps to ensure that any interventions will be both effective and culturally appropriate. Additionally, it is better for interventions to become integrated into systems that are already existing, rather than forcing the refugees to face novel ideas that may seem daunting and culturally irrelevant. Not only does this produce greater participation in the efforts, but it also helps ensure sustainability over the longer term. When in doubt about the direction of a particular intervention, the question should be asked if the efforts are helping to empower the population it is supposed to be serving (Miller & Rasco, 2004).

Significance of the Study

Anyone with a vested interest in the Israeli-Palestinian Conflict will find the research compelling enough to consider. This is primarily a cultural study, so it will be of most interest to those involved in the Israeli-Palestinian Conflict. As the field tries to get a firmer grasp on the way trauma manifests in intergenerational conflicts, it changes the way conflicts are approached. That is to say, it is slowly becoming apparent that the way trauma is understood in the western world may not be completely compatible with the way it manifests in Middle Eastern cultures, or really any non-Western culture for that matter. Without making this study appear more grandiose than it warrants, the idea here is that this study may highlight the assumptions and biases of Western psychology – some erroneous, some not – and declare that Western psychology does not have as much external validity as some may assume. For example, even the understanding of PTSD is challenged by Haj (2015), who noted that the Western psychology definition of trauma is not wholly reflected in the Middle East. A researcher would not use the definition of Dysthymic Disorder to describe Major Depression, and it is similarly nonsensical to use the definition of PTSD as a catch-all for anyone suffering from post-traumatic symptoms.

Finally, this study can add to the current discussion on counterterrorism, which has only recently begun to consider the effectiveness of listening. For many years, most governments' natural response to terrorism has been to fight terrorism with "hard methods," which Pentagon-based counterintelligence special agent Johnson (2017) describes as the one-dimensional mission of killing terrorists. While describing his unit's counterterrorism efforts during Operation Enduring Freedom IX in Afghanistan, Geist (2012) criticizes the overreliance on hard counterterrorism methods as being as abrasive as popping a zit – it is messy, painful, and leaves scars. He explains that the hard method alone is not enough to counteract terrorism because killing a terrorist is often like lawn-mowing a mushroom: "You killed that specific mushroom, but days later, you have a multitude of mushrooms growing right where you chopped the other one down" (p. 153). Indeed, the death of a Muslim is not considered a calamity in Islam because the shedding of martyrs' blood is "a powerful inducement for the Mahdi [Islamic savior] to return to save these faithful believers from destruction" (Shenk, 2007, p. 121).

Geist (2012) and Johnson (2017) argue that the most effective method against terrorism is a combination of hard methods and "soft" methods – winning the hearts and minds of the communities through dialogue and humanitarian assistance. Yom and Saleh (2004) examined the background of 87 Palestinian suicide bombers and concluded that most of them have faced extreme personal trauma (i.e., injury or death of a loved one) at the hands of Israel Defense Forces prior to their volunteering. The reality is that 75% of terrorists have pre-existing social bonds with other extremists before they become terrorists – only an estimated 10% of terrorists are considered loners (Johnson, 2017). Further, most terrorists often do not have bonds with peaceful, sane social networks. Terrorism and peace do not co-exist: people who interact with peaceful communities often are peaceful themselves; when faced with peaceful groups, most terrorists either leave these peaceful communities or eschew their extremist beliefs (Johnson, 2017). Similarly, religious jihadist theology is not a natural progression that appears from studying theology alone, rather there is an already-existing affiliation with a terrorist who espouses jihadist theology. Self-radicalization may not only be rare, but perhaps impossible.

I believe this study to be of significance because of the gap in literature. But much more importantly, this study offers up an outlet for dialogue between Israelis and Palestinians. Unlike governmental proceedings that seek to find compromise, this phenomenological study presents an opportunity for both Israelis and Palestinians to verbalize their experiences. I will not ask any Israeli nor Palestinian to compromise, nor am I seeking a debate regarding who is "right or wrong," as many studies have digressed into: I am seeking to give voice to those who may not have yet had one.

The Impetus

It would feel like an oversight not to acknowledge how this study developed over time. When I was searching for consultants for this a study related to the manifestation of trauma in Israel, I remembered that one of my graduate professors from years earlier was a native-born Israeli who had served in its military before immigrating to the United States. She then received her license in clinical counseling, and years later, taught the craft in a Group Psychotherapy class in which I was a pupil. Her history as an Israeli soldier made an impression on me, and when I asked her to be a consultant for my project, she offered insight that shaped this entire project.

I explained to my former professor that I wanted to research PTSD in Israelis and Palestinians, to which she scoffed that "trauma" in the United States is not equitable to the kind that Israelis and Palestinians face. She described being a child in Israel during the 1960s and 1970s, where she would lie in bed at night and mentally go over scenarios that might happen while she was sleeping. Many of these scenarios were adaptations of other scenarios she had heard other people go through while others were constructed through her own creativity. However, what struck me the most was that my professor had never personally experienced an attack herself, yet she was displaying posttraumatic symptoms that would likely qualify her for a diagnosis if she were in the United States.

My professor explained that her immigration from Israel to the U.S. was not without its interesting set of challenges. For the first two years after her immigration, she faced depression. She chalked this up to being because her body was going through an adrenaline withdrawal, causing her to face a physiological depression in a land where depression is mostly understood from psychological contexts. Israel was much more fast-paced, and being present in the slower-paced United States was actually exhausting as her body depleted itself of the adrenaline.

As I explained what I was seeking to study in Israel, my professor explained that I was carrying too many assumptions that did not translate in this cross-cultural context. I had approached her with an American-bred conceptualization of the historical conflict, to which she challenged as not being accepted by Palestinians. She explained that the very premise of my study (i.e., that Jews were the primary victims of the Holocaust and that the Israeli-Palestinian Conflict is a national war) was disputed. She explained that even the words I was

46

choosing to throw around – like "war" and "trauma" – needed extensive operationalization.

I committed myself to ensuring that my study would not simply become another Americanized conceptualization of the Israeli-Palestinian Conflict, and the following pages hopefully show my efforts towards that commitment. The conversation with my professor had me questioning if PTSD even existed in a Middle Eastern context. What if PTSD is nothing more than physiological depression that is instigated by a surge of adrenaline that does not have a channel to escape once the hose is turned off? This would explain why my professor was dealing with its effects for two years after her immigration, and would explain why most American soldiers do not suffer from PTSD until about 6 months after their return from deployment (Wright et al., 2011; Geist, 2012), and would explain why so few Middle Easterners qualify for a PTSD diagnosis (Haj, 2015).

I knew it was impossible to answer all of the questions I had swirling in my head in just one study. I determined that one of the more accessible questions about my professor's story was this: why did a child – someone who had never personally endured trauma herself – find herself up at night, tormented by these potential scenarios? Something phenomenological was occurring here, and the current literature on PTSD and depression was not sufficing. Thus, I set out to determine if my professor's experience was shared by others and, assuming it was, explore what this construct might be and if Palestinians were also facing it.

Acknowledgement of Personal Bias

Creswell (2013) has outlined the four philosophical assumptions that are present in any qualitative research. The ontological assumption is that qualitative research must embrace the idea that individuals experience different realities and, consequently, there are multiple forms of evidence. The epistemological assumption is that researchers must get as close to their participants as possible to truly understand what it is they are studying, and that evidence will often be subjective because it is based on participants' experiences. The axiological assumption is that researchers have made an honest attempt to become aware of their own biases and accurately report their own values that may be impacting their research, as the researchers' lens will ultimately impact the way a study is conducted and interpreted. Likewise, the methodological assumption is that a researcher's own experiences will shape their research, which is inductive and emergent in nature (meaning that the research's purpose and form may change as data is collected and analyzed).

To me, I conceptualize that information into this idea: researchers are flawed and this means that there exists no perfect study. Even prior to data collection, I had been accused of under-representing the Palestinian narrative by one reader and over-representing the Palestinian narrative by another. I have attempted to tackle a sensitive topic in which not everyone could be satisfied with: even if my study was hypothetically completely devoid of bias (it's not), it is likely that the research would still be criticized as being too one-sided by some readers. So, in light of Creswell's axiological assumption and my conscientiousness as a qualitative researcher, I believe it is my duty to dedicate a small portion of my research to outlining my belief system that is likely impacting my interpretation of this data.

First Bias: Being American

The first bias for me to acknowledge is my ethnicity as an American. In the Israeli-Palestinian Conflict, there are violent offenders within the ranks of both Jews and Arabs. However, Americans are predisposed to viewing only Arabs as the terrorists (Saleem & Anderson, 2013; Jhally, Alper, & Earp, 2016). Saleem and Anderson (2013) conducted a study about this phenomenon and hypothesized that those who play video games in which terrorism is a major theme generally have negative attitudes towards Arabs. Consider the idea that some of the most common enemies in the gaming world are Arab-looking men (i.e., men with turbans, thick beards, and dark skin). Contrast this to the fact there is not a single American-made video game that depicts Israelis or Zionists as terrorists in its storyline. To evaluate their hypothesis, Saleem and Anderson took 224 college-aged Americans and asked about their perceptions of Arabs after randomly assigning them to play one of three video games: a video game in which the enemies were Arab terrorists, a video game in which the enemies were Russian terrorists, or a mini-golf video game that had no enemies. Saleem and Anderson (2013) found that those who played video games depicting Arab terrorists implicitly and explicitly expressed more anti-Arab sentiments than any other group. Participants who played video games depicting Russian terrorists did not have the implicit negative feelings towards Arabs, but did still display explicit negative feelings towards Arabs, suggesting that the media has created deep-seeded associations between terrorism and Arabs. Those who only played the mini-golf game did not have increased negative associations with Arabs.

Palestinians are Arabs, and as such are often lumped together with Islamic extremists. Jhally, Alper, and Earp (2016) go as far as to suggest in their documentary, The Occupation of the American Mind, that Americans have systematically been conditioned to be pro-Israeli, only hearing the Jewish narrative and actually being indoctrinated with falsehoods about Arabs, Palestine, and Hamas. Jhally, Alper, and Earp state that the mark of a biased American is someone who constantly remarks about "Israel's right to defend itself" without actually researching if Israeli attacks were unprovoked or retaliatory. Another mark of bias described by Jhally, Alper, and Earp is that Americans blindly affix the label "terrorism" to Palestinian aggression and refuse to use the same word to describe actions committed by Israel Defense Forces. I admit that these both do describe me. As such, I have to take this assertion very seriously and consider that I may have only been exposed to the pro-Israeli side of the story in my upbringing and therefore have a particular affinity for the Jewish narrative.

The Israeli-Palestinian Conflict is, by definition, a situation in need of conflict resolution (Brueggemann, 2015). Ramsbotham, Woodhouse, and Miall (2011) describe the three schools of thought that have dominated the western view of conflict resolution: those who have the traditional view of conflict resolution tend to conceptualize conflicts as having a protagonist and an antagonist who are vying for power and persuasion; those who have the Marxist view of conflict resolution tend to attempt to reconcile even the most contentious issues by disengaging from finger-pointing and look instead for solutions, rather than fault; finally, those with a realist view of conflict resolution argue that violence is simply an integral part of conflict that must be accepted as a common method of sifting through bellicose issues.

I have adopted all three of these western notions of conflict resolution at different times during my understanding of the Israeli-Palestinian Conflict. I am an American who was raised in a conservative-leaning household, and as such, had generally pro-Israeli sentiments during my critical years. The Second Intifada (2000-2005) took place entirely during my high school years (2001-2005) just as I was forming my political bone, and the Second Lebanon War (2006) and its subsequent fallout occurred at the beginning of my career in the U.S. Army National Guard (2004-2010).

Second Bias: Being Christian

Adding to the pro-Israeli slant that I was exposed to early on, I had a Roman Catholic upbringing and am today an evangelical Christian. As such, this makes me a bit of a fatalist in that I do believe the world has a set expiration date, and I believe that the ancient land of Israel belonged to the Jews, not the Canaanites. While I do not believe the biblical narrative offers a clear-cut argument for who ought to inherit the contemporary land of Israel, I still find myself in defense of Israelis more often than I am in defense of Palestinians, which likely says something about where I would land if forced to identify a protagonist and antagonist in the conflict. (I would prefer not to have to do that.)

An added difficulty is that there is little room for middle ground if we account for religious texts. That is to say, the Jewish and Muslim holy books – almost from start to finish – are in direct contradiction to one another. The Jews contend that Jacob received the birthright from Isaac, while Muslims contend that it was his brother, Esau, who received that inheritance (which would eventually fuel the discussion of who inherited the land of Israel). I naturally accept the historical Jewish narrative as it is a part of the Christian Holy Bible. However, I like to believe that it is not just my bias that leads me to this conclusion, but that there is sense in accepting the Jewish historical narrative over the Muslim historical narrative as it was written far earlier: at its absolute latest, the Hebrew Bible was written

50

no later than the 2nd century BC, while the Islamic holy texts, at their very earliest estimate, were written no earlier than 7th century A.D. Most contemporary scholars contend that the Tanakh was written around 600 B.C. and that the Qur'an was written around 600 A.D., which is a significant enough gap that has led me to trust the Jewish narrative over the Muslim narrative.

Even still, I do not view the Israeli-Palestinian Conflict in such black-and-white terms. When it comes to global affairs, I think that the use of religious texts should be avoided because of the scholarly disagreement regarding the texts' origins, and cannot be used in inter-state conflict resolution to determine which peoples should blindly be allotted certain land. I say this without violating my conscience as a Christian because according to the Jewish Scriptures, God Himself gave the chosen Jewish people into the hands of Arabs time and again. As such, I am forced to acknowledge that even God has not ascribed to the hardline interpretation that the Jews should always control Israel. The Biblical Jews faced consequences for their actions, and this has not changed today. Therefore, my adherence to Christian Scripture does not entice me to necessarily believe that the Jews should be given Israel in diplomatic affairs, only that God has sovereignty and will execute His plans for His chosen people as He sees fit.

Third Bias: Having a Conservative-leaning Foreign Policy

Putting all religious implications aside, I tend to believe that the current land of Israel does, indeed, belong to the Jews and current administration. The situation that arose in 1948 was most tragic: Palestinians, who had long been promised the land of Israel by the British and Ottoman Empires, had this territory stripped away and given instead to a rising enemy who was in need of protection after an annihilation against their race was attempted (Jhally, Alper, & Earp, 2016; Frantzman & Kark, 2013). From a practical and political angle, it seems curious that Jews were given a land that happened to be surrounded by people who had historically been at odds with them, yet this is exactly what occurred.

In response to the abnegation of their promised land, Arabs attempted a coup in 1948. They lost. They recuperated. They staged another well-planned insurrection in 1967, this time with an overwhelming amount of resources and heavy support from each of Israel's bordering neighbors, and they still lost. Other skirmishes have been attempted since then, all with the same result. As such, it strikes me as odd that the global community would expect Israelis to freely relinquish their land to Palestinians any more than it would expect the United States to relinquish its land that it took from the British Empire and from Native Americans. By this logic, should not the United States also forfeit California, Arizona, New Mexico, Nevada, Utah, and Colorado – all land they stole from Mexico during the Mexican-American War? War and violence have always been a natural part of determining land possession, and at the expense of revealing my realist view of conflict resolution, what has happened in the past is just that: history. The following is a controversial statement, but I do not see why Israel should need to give up their borders to what they were prior to 1967, especially because the Six-Day War only helped to support the Israeli narrative that doing so would provide leverage to Israel's enemies to overtake them completely.

This does not mean that modern-day Israel should be excused for their clear violations of international law. As of this writing, Israel has been accused as being incessant aggressors by repeatedly setting up illegal settlements in Palestinian territory (Isaac, 2017). I agree with Steir-Livny's (2016) assessment that the victims have become the bullies. Israeli Prime Minister Netanyahu was secretly recorded in 2001 as saying, "The Arabs are currently focusing on a war of terror and they think it will break us. The main thing, first of all, is to hit them. Not just one blow, but blows that are so painful that the price will be too heavy to be borne. To bring them to the point of being afraid that everything is collapsing" (Jhally, Alper, & Earp, 2016). When pressed on the fact that what he was saying were the actions of a "conqueror" rather than someone just defending his land, Netanyahu defiantly responded, "The world won't say a thing. The world will say we're 'defending.' Especially today, with America. I know what America is: America is something that can easily be moved to the right direction. They won't get in our way. 80% of the Americans support us – it's absurd" (Jhally, Alper, & Earp, 2016).

While I appreciate Israel's age-old claim that they have a right to defend themselves, this argument has been taken too far. It is unfathomable how global action has not been taken against the State of Israel for their settlements, which I view as a crime against humanity. From a Christian perspective and a political perspective, the Israeli offenses against Palestinians are incompatible with my worldview.

If you had previously formed a view on the Israeli-Palestinian Conflict prior to my admission of biases, I can only assume that I have offended you now, regardless of which side you stand on. It is not my intention or focus to pronounce judgment on Israelis or Palestinians, nor is it my goal to point out my worldview. In the most callous sense, I do not care about the Israeli-Palestinian Conflict itself as much as I care about understanding the way trauma manifests through it and the way religion has shaped it. I have not highlighted my biases and beliefs just to vex my reader. Rather, I believe it is not only honest to lay out my worldview to you, but also ethical (Creswell, 2013). I intend not only to refrain from operating off of my biases, but to actively challenge them.

In the end, the Jewish, Christian, and Muslim holy texts all agree on one idea: God will one day establish the true faith. He does not need my help to achieve this.

Summary

Along with an analysis of the Israeli-Palestinian Conflict's political history, Chapter 1 reviewed the need for a study on intergenerational trauma. The proposed study is not without risks. Namely, there is often an implicit notion that religion has no place in psychology. However, it is this notion that has led to the Israeli-Palestinian Conflict not being regarded as holistically as it could be. While the religions of the Israelis and Palestinians do not drive the study (as intergenerational trauma is the focus), religion must be implemented to increase internal validity.

Chapter 2: Current Research on the Topic

Chapter Overview

The following literature review is broken down into two main categories; it includes relevant data 1) as to how religion has impacted the Israeli-Palestinian Conflict, and 2) as to how the Israeli-Palestinian Conflict is understood from a psychological perspective. The first section evaluates the historical contention between Jews and Arabs, the impact religion has on psychological processes, the impact religion has had on international psychology, and the eschatological characteristics that have been hypothesized to influence the sociopolitical landscape of the conflict. The second section evaluates the current state of the field of international psychology, the ethnic collective memories of participants in the Israeli-Palestinian Conflict, the way Jewish victimhood influences the sociopolitical landscape of the conflict, the way terrorism and counterterrorism efforts have impacted the sociopolitical landscape of the conflict, and the current stigma regarding mental health in Israel. This all makes way for a discussion on PTSD in a global context, difficulties in operationalizing trauma across cultures, and, consummately, a discussion of the origins and indications of Transgenerational Trauma Transmission, as well as the way the phenomenon influences those involved in the Israeli-Palestinian Conflict.

To achieve this literature review, queries were made for literature through EBSCO Host, PsycINFO, Google Scholar, and ProQuest. Keywords included trauma, PTSD, post-traumatic growth, psychopathology, transgenerational trauma, vicarious intergenerational trauma, Israeli-Palestinian Conflict, psychology, religion, eschatology, and Magog. Articles that were cited by multiple scholars were given first preference, followed by the most recent date of the article. When a certain author was found to be cited across multiple articles, that author's work was specifically sought out, regardless of the date of the research. All clinical definitions come from either the DSM 5 or the ICD-10 (and were identified each time), and the New International Version (2011) was used as the primary mode of translation for the Holy Bible.

54

Religious Impact on the Conflict

The Unique Element of the Israeli-Palestinian Conflict

The famous story of David and Goliath is a childhood favorite for many, but its prophetic foretelling is perhaps underappreciated. In the biblical book of 1 Samuel, a dispute over land erupts between Israelites and Philistines:

> Goliath stood and shouted to the ranks of Israel, "Why do you come out and line up for battle? Am I not a Philistine, and are you not the servants of Saul? Choose a man and have him come down to me. If he is able to fight and kill me, we will become your subjects; but if I overcome him and kill him, you will become our subjects and serve us." David said to the Philistine, "You come against me with sword and spear and javelin, but I come against you in the name of the Lord Almighty, the God of the armies of Israel, whom you have defied. This day the Lord will deliver you into my hands, and I'll strike you down and cut off your head. This very day I will give the carcasses of the Philistine army to the birds and the wild animals, and the whole world will know that there is a God in Israel. All those gathered here will know that it is not by sword or spear that the Lord saves. (1 Samuel 17:8-9, 45-47)

From the ashes of the Philistines rose the Palestinians as they are known today, and the fighting has not ceased since that epic battle over 3000 years ago. The battle between David and Goliath is the first recorded Israeli-Palestinian altercation in history, and it is also one of the few historical anecdotes that are agreed upon by Jews, Christians, and Muslims alike. It is then perhaps no surprise that the first recorded Israeli-Palestinian dispute was focalized on land.

Of course, disputes over land are not unique. India and Pakistan quarrel over Kashmir; Russia wants complete control of Chechnya from separationists; Kurdish separationists stage uprisings to take control of Iraq (Rydelnik, 2007). What makes the land of Israel so unique is the religious attachments to the land. Indeed, the issue is

55

not so much about the literal land, but what the land means: the land is a religious symbol that continues to regulate the psychological processes of the participants of the Israeli-Palestinian Conflict (Schori-Eyal, Halperin, & Bar-Tal, 2014).

Brueggemann (2015) and Rydelnik (2007), two Christians who fall on opposite sides of the political spectrum in terms of their outlook regarding who shoulders the most responsibility for the failure of peace in the Israeli-Palestinian Conflict, have both indicated that the issue is so overwhelming that neither of them expect a resolution until Jesus Christ comes back to sort the issue out. Perhaps a comical anecdote, but at play here are the larger religious connotations surrounding the Israeli-Palestinian Conflict. Many have attempted to make sense of the conflict without an understanding of the religious symbolism, an effort that is not sufficiently holistic.

Religion in Psychology

Religion has psychological application. Consider scrupulosity, a form of religious obsessive-compulsive disorder (OCD) recognized in the DSM in which the sufferer's religion weaves itself into the intrusive thoughts associated with OCD (Ciarrocchi, 1995). Without a grasp of the way religion and religious thoughts manifest in an OCD-afflicted individual, optimal treatment is unattainable (Huppert, Siev, & Kushner, 2007; Geist, 2016).

Vishkin et al. (2016) considered four past research studies that evaluated 2078 Israelis through religiosity self-reports, the COPE Inventory (to assess coping mechanisms), and the Emotional Regulation Questionnaire. Vishkin et al. found that religious persons were better at cognitive reappraisal and more capable of dealing with trauma than non-religious Israelis. Similarly, Laufer and Solomon (2006) wanted to study the co-existence of PTSD and posttraumatic growth, and ultimately started researching whether or not religion would influence the manifestation of PSG. Laufer and Solomon (2006) solicited 2999 adolescents in Israel – all of whom lived through the Israeli-Palestinian Conflict from 2000 to 2005 – to take the Exposure-to-Terror Questionnaire, conduct self-reported terror accounts, the Child Posttraumatic Stress Reaction Index (CPTS-RI), and the

Posttraumatic Growth Inventory (PTGI). Laufer and Solomon found that religion does play a large role in the manifestation of PSG (i.e., higher religiosity led to higher PSG levels).

The impact of religion is not a phenomenon confined to the people on-ground in Israel. Look no further than the United States' longstanding foreign policy wherein it allies with Israel: the United States, with its large Christian and Jewish presence, has historically been supportive of Israel, even in situations in which Israel has been antagonistic. Just as it has historically been an unspoken understanding that the American president profess to be Christian (Kane & Podell, 2008), it has historically also been an unspoken understanding that the United States will support Israel in political conflicts, largely because the Christian Holy Bible and Jewish Tanakh indicate that Israel has been set aside for Jewish inheritance (Lustick, 1988; Brueggemann, 2015; Shenk, 2007).

Religion in International Psychology

Tarakeshwar, Stanton, and Pargament (2003) asserted that religion is one of the more crucial elements – albeit overlooked – of cross-cultural psychology. In fact, the idea that religion has no place in psychology is a western philosophy that is not as accepted in non-western cultures. For many people, especially those outside of western cultures, religion plays a substantial role in the way people think, feel, perceive the world, and identify themselves (Regnerus & Uecker, 2007). Further, religion has been found to be a predictor of peoples' behavior all over the world and influences multicultural dimensions (Wyshak, 2016; Heim & Schall, 2014; Koenig, Perno, & Hamilton, 2017).

One of the rare areas in psychological literature in which religion is liberally cited is in discussions about terrorism. Understanding the link between terrorism and religion has long been an elusive endeavor, but one tenet that has repeatedly been linked to terror is religious fundamentalism within religions rooted in sacred texts that condone violence (Putra & Sukabdi, 2014). Often, a natural response to this has been to become intolerant towards religions that have texts that seem to justify violence, but Saleem and Anderson

(2013) argue that religious intolerance is actually a self-perpetuating vehicle for terrorism, particularly for Arabs and Muslims in the post-September 11th world.

Munroe and Moghaddam (2012) and Goodwin (2012) explore the dynamics that such religious extremism plays in terrorism. Munroe and Moghaddam make clear that religion does not "cause" terrorism, and that rather the threat of a religion's extinction would instead be the catalyst for terror. Yet, because religion is so closely correlated with terrorism, it ought to be addressed as if it is causal. Goodwin (2012) argues the opposite, that religion cannot be blamed for terrorism, stating that religion is just used as a façade for political agents needing a rallying cry for their cause. As such, Goodwin argues that it makes little sense to blame terrorism on religion when nonreligious factors sufficiently explain the phenomenon. Goodwin's stance is that terrorists use religion to justify – rather than inform – their worldview.

However, religion makes an impact far beyond discussions in terrorism. For one, religious context cannot be separated from the shared experiences of an ethnic group. Tuval-Mashiach and Dekel (2014) conducted narrative interviews of 230 Jewish relocated citizens of Gush Katif (which is in the Gaza Strip). These participants were exiled from their homes in a forced relocation effort in 2005 due to increased violence between Arabs and Israelis (Rydelnik, 2007). The participants' attitudes towards their Jewish faith was specifically examined, and Tuval-Mashiach and Dekel (2014) found one of four general outcomes occurring in each of their interviews: the individuals were resilient to change (i.e., their faith was neither strengthened nor weakened), their faith was strengthened, their faith was weakened, or the participant was in an open crisis (indicating that they were wrestling with what their circumstances meant to their faith). Most relevant, Tuval-Mashiach and Dekel noted that much of the religious meaning-making was actually occurring on a collectivistic level: the current state the participant was in often reflected the greater state of their group as a whole. Thus, the religious meaning-making of an ethnic group cannot be separated from their identity.

Culture and religion are interlinked, as culture influences religious practices whilst religion influences the climate of a particular culture (Tarakeshwar et al., 2003). Of course, when religion and military become intertwined, the end result is often bloodshed (Sabbah, 2015). Sabbah noted that from practical and ethical standpoints alike, the military should never be involved in decisions about whether or not an individual should be allowed to pray. However, by forcing its Palestinian citizens to obtain military permits to attend certain holy places, Israel has accomplished just that. Of course, this is the crux of the Israeli-Palestinian Conflict: for many religious men and women, the land is holy enough to die for, and as a result, many have (Elman, 2016; Sabbah, 2015; Bar-Tal & Halperin, 2014).

It would be easy to dismiss a land dispute as a purely political phenomenon, but the reality is that in the case of the Israeli-Palestinian Conflict: the land dispute is ostensibly a religious dispute (Wyshak, 2016; Shenk, 2007; Schori-Eyal, Halperin, & Bar-Tal, 2014; Cole & Hatano, 2010). It impacts the way trauma manifests and the way non-participating members view the conflict. The meaningfulness of religion to many Israelis and Palestinians cannot be overstated, particularly in the way that religious texts have influenced participants' expectations of how the conflict will play itself out. This can best be exemplified through a brief analysis of the Jewish, Christian, and Islamic religious texts, which hold different interpretations of a specific unfulfilled prophecy about a singular event that is to come.

Gog and Magog: Eschatology of the Israeli-Palestinian Conflict

The religious connotation of Israel being inherited by the Jews has steered American foreign policy since the sovereign state's inception. In fact, Gunter (2015) proclaimed that many American Christians view the establishment of Israel as the fulfillment of several scriptural prophecies, right down to the fact that the Palestinian land was given to Israel by Britain, which is believed to previously be ancient Tarshish:

Surely the coastlands will wait for Me; and the ships of
Tarshish will come first, to bring your sons from afar, their
gold and silver with them, to the name of the Lord your God,
and to the Holy One of Israel, because he has glorified you.
(Isaiah 60:9)

However, if one is to take an apocalyptic interpretation of the
Judeo-Christian books of Daniel, Ezekiel, and Revelation as many
Christians do (Dittmer, 2007; Woodridge, 2006), then it is clear that
the United States will not always be supportive of Israel (Rydelnik,
2007). Scholarly Jews and Arabs alike are cognizant that Israel will
stand alone in a future prophesied battle (Dittmer, 2007; Rydelnik,
2007; Zuhur et al., 2008), and this understanding inevitably permeates
religious Israelis' and religious Palestinians' perception of the Israeli-
Palestinian Conflict.

Scholars of science may feel uncomfortable when terms like
"apocalyptic" or "prophecy" are thrown around in an empirically-
based study. Yet, if not for the religious implications, then at least for
the psychological implications it must be emphasized that all three
Abrahamic religions – Judaism, Christianity, and Islam – agree that a
future prophesied battle concerning Israel is yet to pass (Wyshak,
2016; Shenk, 2007). In the Jewish Scriptures, the city of Damascus –
which boasts of being the oldest continuously inhabited city in the
world – will come to destruction: "An oracle concerning Damascus:
'See, Damascus will no longer be a city but will become a heap of
ruins'" (Isaiah 17:1). This destruction of Damascus will be blamed on
the Jews – it is unclear whether the blame is correctly placed or not –
and will incite the Battle of Gog and Magog.

In short, the Battle of Gog and Magog is an unfulfilled
prophetic battle in all three Abrahamic traditions (Dittmer, 2007;
Rydelnik, 2007; Shenk, 2007). In the Judeo-Christian tradition, a
leader codenamed "Gog" will raise an army – collectively known as
the country of Magog – against Israel. Ezekiel 38-39 of the Jewish
Scriptures and Revelation 20 of the Christian Scriptures detail the rise
of this enemy to Israel, which triggers a war in which so many people
are killed that there will be a need for people whose sole job it is to

amble across Israel, looking for dead bodies to bury. Israel will have no allies in this war, yet will overcome the power of Gog and Magog through the provision of God – very much a macro-retelling of the battle between David and Goliath. In apocalyptic tradition, this battle ushers in the end times in which the Christ returns to judge the world: both the Jewish book of Ezekiel and the Christian book of Revelation establish Israel – or more pointedly, God – as victor, and both accounts detail an astoundingly similar description of a kingdom that will come as a result (Woodridge, 2006; Dittmer, 2007).

In Islamic tradition, the battle of Gog and Magog pans out exactly as just described in the Judeo-Christian tradition, with the exception of one glaring difference: in the Qur'an, Israel will be demolished by Magog, largely made up of Arabs (Dittmer, 2007; Shenk, 2007; Surah Al-Kahf [18]). Israel will be defeated once and for all, and this will marshal in the Islamic Mahdi, who is a savior-figure for Muslims. While there are variations within Islam as to how the end times manifests itself, Muslims generally believe that the Mahdi appears on earth in the last days, heralded in by the sound of a loud trumpet. Mountains crumble as the sky is ripped apart, and all forms of life on earth will be extinguished; only Allah remains for a period. Then a second trumpet sounds, which signifies that all the dead are raised for their judgments. Judgment "day" is estimated to last about 50,000 years, but at the end of it, each individual (Muslim or not) is assigned to one of the eight levels of paradise or to one of the seven levels of hell. Eternity is then consummated with the obliteration of earth, which will have fulfilled its purpose as a testing plane for mankind (Shenk, 2007; Geist, 2012).

While the narrative is unique to Islam, there is some overlap with Christianity. Namely, the Islamic Mahdi will bring with him Jesus of Nazareth, the central figure of Christianity (Molloy, 2013). In Christianity, Jesus Christ appeared as a meek servant who eschewed political leadership in Galilee and instead traveled to Jerusalem so that he could be arrested, beat, and crucified, receiving this brutal punishment as an atonement for mankind, only to resurrect from the dead three days later in a display of God's dominion even over death (Shenk, 2007, p. 121).

61

But for Muslims, Jesus was never crucified: he was taken into heaven by Allah and will return in the role of the annihilator, who destroys Christian and Jewish symbology (including crosses, synagogues, and churches), kills all pigs, and crushes evil men, the anti-Christ, and even Allah's angels as he confirms Islam to be the one true religion (Shenk, 2007, p. 123; Geist, 2012, p. 147).

Rosenberg (2008) argues that it is hard to look at empirical events and not see arresting evidence as to why many religious adherents are wound up about events in the Israeli-Palestinian Conflict today. Rosenberg points out that such an apocalyptic battle could not have taken place before the current escalation between Jews and Arabs because of three factors. First, the Old Testament prophet, Daniel, explains that in the last days (i.e., that which precedes the Battle of Gog and Magog), there will be a surge of increase in knowledge (Daniel 12:4). Rosenberg argues that the emergence of the Internet is the first invention that has made this possible. Secondly, Rosenberg points out that in the passages of Ezekiel that just precede the Battle of Gog and Magog, it is prophesied that Israel's people will re-inhabit their land, which clearly is compatible with the creation of the State of Israel in 1948. Finally, Ezekiel hints at the use of nuclear weapons in the Battle of Gog and Magog, which, again, was not possible until the modern day: "I will pour down torrents of rain, hailstones and burning sulfur on him and on his troops and on the many nations with him" (Ezekiel 38:18-22).

Ishmael, the firstborn of Abraham and heir-apparent to the land of Israel, is regarded by Muslims as their Abrahamic ancestor. The context of his birthright is debated between Jews and Muslims today, and has context recorded back as far as the Book of Genesis. One does not need to fully believe in these prophecies to at least appreciate the way the religious texts influence the Israeli-Palestinian Conflict, which cannot be brushed off as purely a political conflict. It must also be noted that the aforementioned aspects are nothing more than a primer on the issue, and that the relevance to religious texts go way beyond what has been presented here.

Religious scholars in favor of the Jews maintaining control of Jerusalem point out that the Hebrew Bible mentions the holy city of Jerusalem 669 times, while the Qur'an mentions the holy city exactly zero times. Yet, proponents of a Muslim-controlled Jerusalem argue that the Muslim occupancy of Israel predates the Jews' occupancy: in Jewish tradition, when Joshua takes control of the land of Israel for the first time in Jewish history, he does not drive out the Canaanites who were already dwelling in the land, and instead puts these Canaanites to forced labor under the Jews (Joshua 17:13). Today, some Muslims argue that the original Canaanites were Arabs, and use this argument for why they – not the Jews – are the rightful owners of the land of Israel (Shapiro & Goldberg, 2002). Jews vehemently refute the validity of these claims, and scholars concede that such ancient issues cannot be known for sure: the Hebrew Bible was written prior to 500 B.C., and the Qur'an is as old as A.D. 609. As such, some scholars argue that the Israeli-Palestinian Conflict should only be considered from a modern context, despite this religious interplay.

The religious undertones are important, however, to both the priest and to the scientist. The literal land of Israel is a religious symbol: Jews want the land back because they believe it is inherently theirs, Christians want the Jews to have the land back to herald in the end times and the return of the Christ, and Muslims want the land as it will establish Islam as the holy and true religion of the world. While these religious connotations are lost on many participants of the Israeli-Palestinian Conflict, it cannot be ignored that there are some that are at least somewhat fueled by these religious markings, which equips both Jews and Arabs to endure unspeakable trauma amidst the conflict.

Psychological Impact on the Conflict

The State of the Field of Psychology

Theories from western psychologists are often rooted in Cartesian philosophy that mind and body are separate entities (i.e., one does not affect the other). As a result, many somatic expressions of distress are regarded as psychological deficiency, and causes gaps in values, beliefs, and expectations between doctors and their patients, which in turn, causes treatment plans to be not adhered to (Sorel, 2013).

Stevens (2007) suggested that reductionist Cartesian psychology is being replaced by alternative psychology, which offers more holistic approaches than what have been used in the past. In the past, mainstream psychology has been driven with the assumption that any cognitive process in the brain can be empirically measured. Alternative psychology, however, emphasizes the importance of meaning-making and analyzing culture in context-specific ways. In fact, Marsella (2013) posited that psychology in its entirety is only a reflection of the indigenous community that it originated from, quashing the notion that there is a "Global Psychology" that all cultures adhere to.

The "why" of psychology is becoming less favored over the "how" in psychology. Stevens (2007) highlighted that researchers have until the end of time to figure out "why" something is happening, but it is in understanding the "how" that is time-dependent and can practically save lives. Therefore, Stevens said that there is a greater call for preventing a phenomenon from happening rather than understanding its etymological roots. Both are certainly important, but only one of them has a direct impact on peoples' suffering.

It is for this reason, and under this direction, that the focus of this research was mindful of being practical and relevant to the Israeli-Palestinian Conflict specifically. Internal validity was of much more importance than external validity, and the aim of this study was not to offer an axiom that can be generalized across the globe, but to offer insight as to how trauma manifests in the Israeli-Palestinian Conflict and offer solutions to help increase reconciliation efforts.

The field of psychology often carries a western connotation. The concept of international psychology is more inclusive of non-western cultures and, specifically, how their cognitive processes work differently than those in western cultures. Stevens (2012) explored the existence of psychological principals in 35 countries in terms of the countries' ability to produce scholarly articles and existence of psychological ethics codes. Stevens obtained data on population, urban population, economic and political freedom, Human Development Index, Internet users, psychologists per capita, authors of scholarly articles, scholarly journals, and psychological associations within the countries. Using exploratory factor analyses, Stevens found that the more economic and political freedom a country possessed, the more likely it was to also possess a grip on standard psychological practices. Interestingly, urban population was an even higher predictor than political freedom.

While neither Israel or Palestine were specifically included in the study, the generalizability of this research appeared to be expansive (Stevens, 2012). The idea that a politically hostage country has less of a grasp on psychological concepts suggests that any study within Israel or Palestine – two countries perpetually struggling for freedom from political instability – will need special attention to operationalization of concepts. The principles of trauma, cognition, and intergenerational effects are not as inherently understood from the outset.

Ethnic Collective Memories

One of the psychological challenges to the Israeli-Palestinian Conflict is that there is disagreement about the premises that drive the conflict. Even in contemporary schools, the subject of the Israeli-Palestinian Conflict is a sensitive topic with a contested history. Gross and Gamal (2014) conducted qualitative interviews on three Arab-Israeli teachers with an average of over 30 years of teaching experience. Using grounded theory five-stage analysis, the researchers found that the history being taught by Israelis was biased against Palestinians, whose oppression has been minimized. Conversely, in Shapiro and Goldberg's 2002 documentary <u>Promises</u>, one Arab educator at the Faith Islamic Boys' School holds up a picture of a deer.

"This deer, does it like freedom or captivity?" the educator asks, to which the children reply with the former. "Freedom: good. Do you like freedom?"

"Yes," the children cry out.

"Do the children of Palestine live in freedom?" the educator asks, changing his inflection.

"No," the children shout.

"Are you free like the deer? Or is something obstructing your freedom, like the people who are prevented from going to pray in Jerusalem? Can someone draw a picture that shows how you feel?"

One Palestinian child draws a child holding a stone with the caption, "I will kill them," while another child in the illustration is captioned as saying, "They killed my mother, father, and sister; may God curse them."

After asking the children to draw pictures of their persecution, the Arab educator reviews with the children, "What does our religion say? Who does Jerusalem belong to?"

Children respond with a variety of responses, including "the Palestinians," "the Canaanites," or "the Muslims."

Neither the three Muslim-ascribing teachers from Gross and Gamal's study (2014) nor the singular Muslim teacher from Shapiro and Goldberg's documentary (2002) are a sizeable enough sample to draw any significant conclusions about this particular topic. However, it is not uncommon for such collective memories to drastically differ: an even more pronounced instance of this occurs when discussing the Ottoman Empire's systematic killing of Armenians in 1915. Armenians contend that they were needlessly annihilated by the Turks during World War I (Bulut, 2017). Meanwhile, the Turkish collective memory is that these killings were a natural part of civil war (Republic of Turkey, 2011), and some Turks even contend that the Armenians were the ones slaughtering the Turks (Bulut, 2017).

There even lacks a consensual agreement on the numbers of deaths during this period: scholars have claimed that approximately 1.75 million Armenians were slaughtered in what they refer to as a "genocide" (Kifner, 2007), while the official stance from Turkey is that, at most, 600,000 Armenians were killed in what they refer to as "civil war" (Republic of Turkey, 2011) – a disparity of over 1,000,000 people. Obviously, these narratives are wildly opposite from one another, and finding the specific figures and truth of a narrative becomes a quagmire in itself. For instance, there is not even agreement among Jews of how many perished in the Holocaust: while many Jewish estimates put the count at 6,000,000, many others believe that this number even is curtailed by at least 1,500,000, citing the efforts of Father Patrick Desbois, who claims to have found nearly 3,000 mass graves of unaccounted Jew Holocaust victims (Desbois, 2009; Braverman, 2017). As such, the Sisyphean task of determining the historical accuracy of any presented facts was not pursued in this study. Instead, grasping the general collective memory – a much more attainable venture – was the goal.

Victimhood in a Jewish Context

There exists yet another psychological concept that only muddies the complexity of the Israeli mindset: victimhood. The Holocaust adds a rare (if not unique) attribute to the Jewish race and the way they process conflict, and the historical systematic genocide of the Jewish race adds a complicating psychological phenomenon.

It is important to understand victimhood in the context of the past and present. Schori-Eyal, Halperin, and Bar-Tal (2014) noted two distinct types of victimhood: historical and conflict. Historical victimhood connotes a shared cultural identity with others due to a specific event in history, while general conflict victimhood is a shared identity in relation to a specific event going on currently. While Arabs see the Holocaust and the modern-day Israeli-Palestinian Conflict as largely unrelated events, Jews merge these two events into one collective victimhood, spurring modern-day defense of Israel essentially as a response to the Holocaust.

The Holocaust has prompted some Jews to take the stance that in order to avoid becoming victims again (as they were in the Shoah), an aggressive Zionist view must be taken. Omeish and Omeish (2006) argue that it is this Zionism that is the cause of the Israeli-Palestinian

Conflict, not Judaism or Islam. Israeli human rights lawyer Allegra Pacheco states that "criticizing the Israeli government policy for assassinating people or for shooting children and maiming them for thousands of children, that's not anti-Semitic, that's humane" (Omeish & Omeish, 2006). Unfortunately, those who disagree with the Zionist stance are often labeled anti-Semitic, and anti-Zionism has now been paired with anti-Semitism (Scham, 2015). The rise of Islam and the rise of anti-Semitism have indeed gone hand-in-hand: as Palestine became more Islamic in nature, so has it become anti-Semitic (Lipstadt, 1993).

Of course, this collective victimhood is not confined to the events of the Holocaust. Birnbaum (2008) states that even the ancient Israelis found identity in their suffering, and many of them may have actually been suffering from what would be considered PTSD-like symptoms today.

Keret (2016) posed a unique analogy in considering the Israeli-Palestinian Conflict. Using personal autoethnography, Keret argued that the term "pro-" is reductive and, frankly, results in silly labels. Keret stated that considering oneself "pro-Israel" or "pro-Palestinian" is not unlike indulgent fans of American football, who commit to a favorite team and then blindly throw their support behind that team, embracing even the most illogical arguments if the argument favors their beloved team. Keret wishes these labels ought to be tossed to the wayside in favor of becoming "pro-innocent-lives." That is, when a pro-Israel person reads about the Israeli military needlessly killing a Palestinian, the pro-Israel person will put aside his or her affiliations and denounce Israel's actions. Unfortunately, Keret's thought is idealistic and, to his point, can feel as daunting as it would be for a New York Yankee fan to support the Boston Red Sox in the World Series.

Of course, the denial (or at least the minimization) of the Holocaust only serves to fuel the Jewish race into feeling victimized further, prompting them to take extreme measures against their enemies: Israel has been known to consistently break international law by setting up occupation settlements outside of their legal territories

(Lustick, 1988; Isaac, 2017; Rydelnik, 2007; Omeish & Omeish, 2006; Jhally, Alper, & Earp, 2016). Through a worldly lens, this is contemptible because it breaks the law. From a victimhood lens, this is necessary to preempt enemy strikes.

The Palestinians were promised by the 1948 UN General Assembly Resolution 194 that any Palestinian refugees desiring to return to their homeland may do so if they live at peace with their neighbors (Rydelnik, 2007). In 1948 when this promise was made, there were 873,000 Jews and less than 350,000 Palestinian refugees; today, there are 6.5 million Jews in Israel, but also an estimate of an amount nearly equal to that of Palestinian refugees (Katz & Lavee, 2004). In fulfillment of UN General Assembly Resolution 194, Israel would cease as a Jewish state: adding the Palestinians to the already-existent number of Arabs in Israel would significantly outnumber the Jews. Add to this the psychological component of victimhood, and Israelis insist that the overwhelming Arab population would annihilate the Jewish race. Indeed, Palestinians claim their right to return to their land as promised by the UN. But for the Jews through their lens of victimhood, this land is the only bargaining chip left for their chance at peace and self-preservation.

Terrorism in an Israeli-Palestinian Context

Terrorism studies have increasingly become in vogue in western psychology. Ironically though, most of the terrorism in the world occurs in non-western contexts (Butler, 2001). In one study, Graham and Chattopadhyay (2009) argue that terrorism has become so commonplace in many non-western locations around the world that it is an *expected* event to happen at some point. This acceptance of deadly violence as just a natural part of life had helped Afghans to cope with terrorism, and actually made them *happier* than other populations who were actively trying to circumvent terrorism before it happened. While Afghanistan is in Southwest Asia, the principle seems to extend its validity to Middle Eastern contexts as well (Graham & Chattopadhyay, 2009).

It has been proposed that perhaps terrorists are motivated to engage in terror mainly because of their poverty (Butler, 2001), but this is perhaps another western notion. Studies by Berrebi actually came to the opposite conclusion. In fact, McCallister and Schmid (2013) have formulated that most Palestinian suicide bombers and other terrorists are generally above the poverty level and have a significantly higher level of education and higher rate of employment than the average population of Palestinians (see Table 3). Of 335 suicide bombers studied by Berrebi, only 16% had income rated below the poverty level. However, approximately 31% of Palestinians are considered to be below the poverty level. Therefore, if education or socioeconomic statuses were a primary factor that breeds terrorism in Israel, then there would actually be fewer Palestinian terrorists than what is true. McCallister and Schmid (2013) note that this pattern is also seen when the peaceful Lebanese population is compared to violent members of Hezbollah. These figures suggest that socioeconomic factors are non-factors, or perhaps even negatively correlated with terrorism.

TABLE 3: Berrebi's studies on Palestinian education level and correlation with terrorism (McCallister & Schmid, 2013)

Average Palestinian Population	vs. Berrebi's study of 100 extremists
51% have a high school diploma	96% had high school diploma
15% have higher education	65% had higher education
69% have employment	94% had employment

An important limitation to note about these studies is that the study of terrorists is a very difficult and elusive task. The very act of selecting a sample of "terrorists" comes under heavy scrutiny because it is hard to gauge the true motivation behind terrorism, especially when most of that sample has been killed, which is the case for terrorists (McCallister & Schmid, 2013). Additionally, there is no agreed-upon operationalized line between what constitutes a political activist versus an extreme fanatic; or, as the anonymous adage goes, "One man's freedom fighter is another man's terrorist" (Butler, 2001).

Regardless of the reason one becomes a terrorist, when one commits to a life of violence, it is rare for that to be reversed (Johnson, 2017). Moghaddam (2005) describes the global phenomenon of terrorism as a staircase that narrows at the top. The reality is that most "potential terrorists" – that is, people who have a negative impression of a certain group of people or have been wronged by the majority – will never become full-blown terrorists. Most likely, they will stay at the bottom of the staircase; only a few stragglers will ever make it to the top. However, once they reach that second rung of the staircase, it is often fruitless to attempt to convince them to change their ideology: they are set in their beliefs and are unlikely to change. Therefore, it is usually not beneficial to go after those who have begun to ascend the staircase. It has been for this reason that global governments are urged to focus their policies on those still on the ground (i.e., those who have not begun to climb Moghaddam's "staircase of terrorism"). Pursuing the psychological reversal of a terrorist is often futile, but establishing democracy on the ground floor may eventually dismantle the staircase.

In a cruel irony, those who begin to climb the staircase of terrorism are often not the ones who suffer the worst for their actions. UNICEF estimates that over 80% of victims of war are women and children who have been "deliberately targeted" by those engaging in terrorism and warfare (Yule et al., 2003, p. 217). If nearly 100% of the terrorists in the Israeli-Palestinian Conflict are men, then this indicates that those who are causing nearly 100% of the damage are only suffering 20% of the consequences.

Obviously, these acts of terror greatly impact its victims and sometimes embolden them to become terrorists themselves. The decision to commit a terrorist act is usually preceded by a trauma that the victim believes needs to be avenged (Auerhahn & Laub, 1998). Surprisingly, the violent act that the individual wants to avenge is often a trauma that has not happened to them personally. Instead, the trauma was inflicted upon their parents or siblings and the individual has internalized that trauma vicariously as if they endured it themselves. Therefore, terrorism does not die when the terrorist dies. Conversely, the ideals of that terrorist live on through an intergenerational memory. Auerhahn and Laub (1998) have emphasized the way the Holocaust has made *all* Jews into victims by way of their collective memory. This mentality has fueled the Zionist platform within the Israeli-Palestinian Conflict, and this rhetoric has manufactured terrorists on both sides of the conflict. These terrorists believe in repaying evil with evil, even if the ones who were the impetus for the initial evil have been dead for centuries.

Negative Stigma of Discourse Regarding Mental Health in Israel

The Middle East is resistant to western notions of psychology for political and apolitical reasons alike (Dardas & Simmons, 2015). Despite this, Israel stands as a country that has largely accepted western thinking in terms of medical (including mental health) advancements. Further, Israel has already developed a psychological code of ethics in the nation's short existence as a recognized sovereign state by the United Nations (Welfel & Khamush, 2012). In many ways, Israel remains competitively competent with superpowers like the United States and European countries.

However, stigma still affects Israel's mental health policy and practices, making it sometimes difficult to analyze. The psychological, sociological, and cultural manifestations and implications of stigma in Israel are not unlike what U.S.-based psychologists see play out in the western world. Struch et al. (2008) explored the stigma experienced by mental health service users by examining 167 adults in outpatient treatment in Israel. Of the participants, about two-thirds had been hospitalized at some point in their lifetime for mental illness. During interviews, most participants reported that they had experienced rejection in some form or another as a direct result of their mental illness. To combat this rejection, some of the common coping mechanisms used included education (both going to school and informal learning), withdrawal (unhealthy mechanism), secrecy (i.e., not telling others about their struggles), and positive distinctiveness (i.e., reframing their mental illness as a strength instead of a weakness). Participants generally agreed that in this context, an awareness of the reality of stigma was the solution, indicating that education efforts would be an effective means to dispel stigma.

From a historical and/or human rights perspective, breaking down stigma in Israel is tougher than in a country like the United States, where a general American identity is espoused by its citizens. Specifically in Israel, there are the two dominant cultural communities: Jews (or Israelis) and Arabs (or Palestinians). Dardas and Simmons (2015) note that this cultural identity difference is a division point in Israel that also seeps into the way stigma plays out in the nation.

Like in the United States, nursing techniques in Israel are holistic in nature and patient-centered (Dardas & Simmons, 2015). Not shockingly, stigma is considered the top factor as to why those who need the most help do not seek care. For both Jews and Arabs, the stigma of the mentally ill being "weak" is a large obstacle barring the ill from getting the treatment they need. Further, anti-western sentiment is strong in the Arab community, and this only serves to further solidify the resistance to treatment, as treatment is often associated with western theory. A final factor to consider is that resources are generally scarce in most Middle Eastern countries anyway, though Israel is actually an exception to this rule. Yet, these resources have largely been made available with the help of the United States which, again, creates a barrier to anti-western Israelis or Palestinians who need treatment but refuse to seek it on principle of boycotting western thought.

Israel is also similar to the United States in that stigma is highest in poor or under-resourced areas (Sorel, 2013). Communities with the least amount of resources (including instruments) are the ones hit hardest by misinformation about mental health. Pescosolido et al. (2013) note that levels of recognition, acceptance of biological causes, and public approval of typical treatments are high across the globe, and yet, prejudices remained in these same communities in which misinformation was minimal. Tomlinson and Lund (2012) note that there is not a great deal of visibility in the combatting of mental disorders and stigma, which results in less policy attention and funding, which then results in weaker diagnostic standards and instruments. As it stands, Israel uses the same diagnostic tools as any of the European countries, referring to the ICD-10 for diagnoses.

Israel is currently one of five countries (the others being Japan, Austria, Netherlands, and Germany) to have long-term care insurance (LTCI) (Strier & Werner, 2016). Simply described, LTCI is home-based care that is provided by society that is geared to help those without medical resources. Past studies have shown that LTCI indeed helps improve the quality of life (particularly for the elderly and those who are sick), and yet few Israelis take advantage of this program because of stigmas from both the Israeli citizens and the nurses who are responsible for assessing eligibility (Strier & Werner, 2016). Tal, Roe, and Corrigan (2007) found that while there existed community-based agencies providing rehabilitation in Israel, there were little to no efforts to educate the general public about mental illness, truncating the eradication of stigma.

As with any country – developed or not – there are challenges of integrating mental health care amidst the sting of stigma. An Israeli study conducted by Arikan, Uysal, and Cetin (1999) evaluated the attitudes of 700 students in their final year of university. The students filled out the Dangerousness Scale, a questionnaire devised to evaluate how dangerous mental illness is perceived by its takers. The students specifically outlined whether or not they felt mental illness was a treatable condition, and whether mental illness was dangerous. The study found that those who said that most or all mental illness is treatable also had attitudes that reflected that they believed that the mentally ill were not any more particularly dangerous than those without mental illness. Conversely, those who believed that mental illness was not easily treatable also tended to believe that mentally ill people were more dangerous than healthy people.

Interestingly, these results were not confined to university students, but also health professionals. Artzi-Medvedik, Chertok, and Romem (2012) also conducted a study regarding nurses' attitudes towards mentally ill women breastfeeding. As for some background, mothers' milk is generally considered to be the healthiest choice for infants (as opposed to formula), and the attitudes of nurses often play an important role in educating new mothers about whether or not they should breastfeed their young. Further, the milk of mentally ill women poses no more risk than a healthy woman. Yet, this study found that only 70% of the nurses ($N = 110$, which were a combination of midwives, psychiatric, and postpartum nurses) had positive feelings about allowing schizophrenic women to breastfeed their babies.

These studies underline the barriers for mental health discussions in Israel. Additionally, these studies highlight that stigma is very much a phenomenon that permeates peoples' mindsets, even people who are health professionals. As such, it is critical to understand that conversations about mental illness are still a sensitive subject that is difficult for many Israelis and Palestinians to openly discuss, despite the common frequency of trauma and trauma-based mental illness.

PTSD in a Global Context

In the past, there have been disastrous consequences when attempts have been made to apply western psychological concepts to non-western settings (Watters, 2010). Those who live in peaceful countries have a different understanding of war than those who experience it daily (Vered & Bar-Tal, 2014). A westerner may define war as a period of political unrest that results in temporary bloodshed for as long as it takes to reach a resolution to the conflict. Yet for someone living in Israel or Palestine today, their entire life has been marked by political unrest, bloodshed, and resolution failures. The westerner must go "over there" to find war; the Israeli and the Palestinian simply must walk out of their home to be immersed in it.

In a study conducted with 17 qualitative interviews, Vered and Bar-Tal (2014) found that the concept of conflict was markedly different for Israelis and Palestinians than it was for outsiders. Aspects of daily Israeli life – most specifically, the presence of guns in toy shops, bunkers built-in to business buildings, security checkpoints, aircrafts constantly flying overhead, crude language, and hyper-situational awareness – were startling to outsiders, yet were normal phenomena for Israelis and Palestinians.

Nadan and Ben-Ari (2015) likewise conducted 25 qualitative interviews in Israel and found that the state of hostility permeates every aspect of life in Israel, even the concept of what being "well-adjusted" means. Startlingly, many social work concepts have not been studied in the context of perpetual conflict, and there is little direction for a social worker who finds himself/herself operating in a combat zone. Nadan and Ben-Ari unearthed four themes that appeared for social workers in an area in political conflict that are not reflected in peaceful areas. First, an "us vs. them" mentality exists for most of those who find themselves in political conflict. Secondly, the specter of war permeates even the most innocent of places – one participant in this study found that she cannot even teach basic lessons to a mixed classroom of Jews and Arabs without fear of causing conflict between the students. Additionally, it is nearly impossible to divorce one's political feelings from their professional requirements, and doing so is mentally and emotionally exhausting due to the amount of intentional awareness it requires. Finally, conducting social work amidst a political conflict almost manifests as an oxymoron: how might a social worker execute his/her responsibilities without being able to speak to the social climate of the state? How can the social worker succeed in an environment where the social and the political are intertwined?

Canetti et al. (2016) studied PTSD in an Israeli-Palestinian context. They argue that, while a "trauma" component is necessary for a diagnosis of PTSD, trauma itself is not enough to characterize the disorder: those who develop PTSD are predisposed to it through their personality traits and ability of cognitive control. Studying 256 Israelis and 514 Palestinians ($N = 770$) who have been exposed to trauma in the Israeli-Palestinian Conflict, each participant's vulnerability to PTSD, exposure to trauma, and gender were analyzed. Each participant took a set of five questionnaires that assessed demographics, trauma, PTSD symptoms, cognitive thought strategies, and personality traits, and then the results from those questionnaires were put through path analysis. The researchers concluded that PTSD vulnerability increases in the face of violence that stems from political factors, as political factors increase the stress of the trauma. Further, it was revealed that introverts (as opposed to extroverts) and emotionally unstable personalities were particularly susceptible to PTSD and depression, especially in the Palestinian population. The researchers argue that a more aggressive approach to mitigating PTSD in these populations may help to reduce violence, as those who suffer trauma are more likely to propagate it in the future. That is, trauma promulgates trauma.

Haj (2015) laid groundwork for this current research in that she examined the acute way that trauma affects non-westerners. Using a mixed methods design, Haj studied the types of trauma that Arabs face, the symptoms that are specific to Arabs, and whether or not the Western definition of PTSD is congruent with the way trauma manifests in the Middle East. She found that each of her participants manifested symptoms of trauma, including the typical fear, stress, and disturbances that are generally associated with PTSD. Yet, only six of the 23 participants met diagnosis for PTSD based on Western criteria. While her study had a small sample size, the suggestion was that the clinical definition of PTSD is perhaps more stringent than is seen in other countries.

It is important to be cognizant of the fact that the term PTSD carries a western connotation to it, and is probably an inappropriate term to use for the purposes of this study. PTSD can sometimes only be diagnosed after an individual is removed from the distressing trauma, of which Israelis and Palestinians cannot be characterized by as they are experiencing ongoing trauma. Despite their immersion in traumatic stress, many Israelis and Palestinians therefore would not qualify for a diagnosis of PTSD if DSM criteria are to be used.

Even the broad concept of "war" in a western context may manifest differently in a non-western context. For instance, citizens of the United States have only understood war as a phenomenon that occurs on foreign soil. For an American, "war" may bring up images of the Civil War or incidents like the attack on Pearl Harbor, but for those in the Middle East, war is a regular occurrence – not on foreign soil, but on their own. Further, any non-Vietnam-draft-era United States citizen who finds himself/herself in war has done so as a direct result of personal choice. This is not true for those in other countries. Both Israelis and Palestinians are *de facto* drafted into war just by being residents of Israel. There is no escaping war as it is an inherent part of the identity of each and every Israeli and Palestinian.

The complexities of the Israeli-Palestinian Conflict transcend modern trauma-based DSM diagnoses (Ayer et al., 2015). The conflict itself forces its participants to reframe the way they understand trauma, as the experience of trauma in the Israeli-Palestinian Conflict not only comes with the typical distressing symptoms, but also impacts participants' attitudes towards groups of different religions and their opinion on peace and war. Unfortunately for Palestinians specifically, the lower one's socioeconomic status, the more extensive is one's psychological distress (Ayer et al., 2015).

Dickstein et al. (2011) posited that there has not been enough research on trauma in contexts where there is a constant threat of terrorism. To study this phenomenon, the researchers used exploratory factor analysis on the coping abilities of Israelis who lived along the Gaza border. A total of 1850 telephone calls were placed, each participant's number being used via stratified sampling. Of those called, 24.3% successfully completed the researchers' interview ($N =$ 450). Using moderation analysis, three of the seven factors studied – substance use coping, denial/disengagement, and social support – showed that such mechanisms increased psychological functioning in the face of terror. One of the factors (i.e., acceptance/positive reframing) helped to mitigate distress. The primary conclusion from this study is that psychological coping mechanisms need to be contextually based. That means that understanding psychological coping looks much different in a war-torn country than it would in a country that has known much peace. The psychological development of individuals in these countries-in-turmoil is inherently going to be different than those who do not know political conflict.

Hobfoll et al. (2009) felt there was a gap in research that contemplates longitudinal resilience and resistance for those in threat of mass casualty (i.e., those facing a war or conflict). To remedy this, the authors researched this phenomenon by using stratified sampling to select 709 Jews and Arabs, though a glaring limitation of this study is that the breakdown between how many of the 709 participants were

Jews and how many were Arabs is not present. However, all of the participants lived through a time of terrorist attacks between 2004 and 2005. The researchers studied each participant's terrorism exposure level, loss of economic and psychosocial resources, posttraumatic growth, social support, PTSD, and depression using logistic regression.

Hobfoll et al. (2009) defined resilience as the ability to cope amidst chaos, and defined resistance as an ability to defy distressing feelings in the midst of chaos. It was found that direct terrorism exposure did not necessarily affect resilience or resistance. The study suggested that males and Jews have a better level of resistance and resilience than others, and those without support systems were at highest risk to being permanently affected by trauma. In terms of my research, this may suggest that Jews as an ethnic majority are perhaps better positioned to survive a long-term conflict. With fewer resources, Arabs would likely "lose" the conflict if there were no outside intervention at any time. Additionally, the idea that the conflict must be examined holistically – to include resilience and resistance – is supported by the findings here.

While a holistic lens is certainly necessary (especially when the impetus for conflict is a friction of different cultures and religions), Obeidi (2014) warned that research should not become overambitious. He notes that several attempts to solve the macro-problem of the Israeli-Palestinian Conflict at large have been made, and all have failed. As a result, there exists a pessimism concerning grassroots organizations, which have often halted attempts towards peace. Therefore, a new lens in considering the Israeli-Palestinian Conflict should be used, and that lens is examining the conflict from a micro-level angle that tackles one aspect of the conflict, rather than trying to take on the whole conflict at once.

Operationalizing Pathological Trauma

The purpose of this research is to be a component of the micro-level research suggested by Obeidi (2014). Specifically, the way trauma manifests on an intergenerational level will be the focus going forward. The aforementioned research warrants a reframing of the term PTSD in context of the Israeli-Palestinian Conflict. PTSD is a diagnosis best kept in the west, as its criteria are not culturally congruent with areas that experience incessant trauma (Haj, 2015). A prerequisite of a delayed PTSD diagnosis requires the traumatic event to have been concluded. If one were to eliminate this component and call it "combat stress reaction," this would allow those concurrently in trauma to qualify for the diagnosis. However, the complexity rises even above this as a proposed "combat stress reaction" diagnosis would not account for the intergenerational aspect that is such a major theme of the Israeli-Palestinian Conflict.

Straker (2013) offered the term Continuous Traumatic Stress (CTS), which is more inclusive of those who suffer trauma on a regular basis over a prolonged period of time. Straker predicated her research on the assertion that CTS was developed in response to civil conflict in South Africa's movement against apartheid. CTS requires systematic conflict to be present as opposed to a series of acute incidents. In Straker's research, she noted that 98.9% of South Africans living in Cape Town had personally witnessed violence against their community, and it is with this systematic reality that CTS was possible.

The elements of trauma within the Israeli-Palestinian Conflict overlap with the violence in South Africa's history. Of course, CTS as described by Straker (2013) is clearly observable in Israelis and Palestinians. However, the situation is confounded when the longevity of the conflict is taken into account. There is perhaps no modern conflict that has the unique history that can be found in the Israeli-Palestinian Conflict. As will be explored here, there is a unique onset of trauma in which those who have never personally experienced trauma themselves manifest trauma-like symptoms just by hearing stories of traumatic situations from family members. What is being discussed is *not* complex trauma, which is defined as when a victim is in a repetitively negative situation that does not qualify as a truly traumatic experience, and is characterized by excessive rumination (Courtois, 2004). Instead, this particular trauma refers to those who operate as if they are living under a post-trauma life despite having only been told secondhand stories of such trauma.

LaCapra (2001) asserts the obvious notion that trauma sufferers often need outside help in working through trauma they face. LaCapra described that trauma sufferers can head down one of two roads: they will either *act out* as a result of their trauma, or they can *work through* the trauma. Those who *act out* relive a past trauma concurrently in the present and use their traumatic experience to fuel negative behavior, specifically through uncontrollable repetition, as if the trauma is still going on. Conversely, those who *work through* trauma are able to overcome the negative effects of the trauma by distancing the trauma from the self. While the individual cannot completely disengage from the trauma, the individual can at least differentiate between the past and the present, allowing him/her to better control the negative impact of the trauma. While LaCapra never goes into depth in this article regarding intergenerational trauma, it can be supposed that those who indoctrinate fear into their offspring or protégés are *acting out*.

Perhaps the greatest contributor to the study of intergenerational trauma is Marianne Hirsch, who coined the phrase *postmemory*. Hirsch's idea is that harsh memories come after the traumatic memory, or literally the "memory after the memory." In this sense, the trauma is not an actual event, but rather, the passed-down retelling and/or memory of the event is where the heart of the trauma remains. Postmemory is named after similar *post-* verbiage, such as *postmodern* or *postcolonial*, which implies that there is a continuous connection between the critical past and the modern time (Hirsch, 2008). In some of her earlier research, Hirsch actually studied the intergenerational trauma that manifests in the Israeli-Palestinian Conflict. Hirsch describes a second generation of Holocaust survivors (i.e., children of Holocaust sufferers) whom are so influenced by their parents' tragedy that it is almost as if the second generation personally lived through the trauma (Hirsch, 1997). Despite having been born long after the Holocaust ended, these children inherit the tragedy (and subsequent PTSD-like symptoms) into their own biography.

This has lasting implications as it means that anyone who recognizes the Holocaust as a central trauma in history is potentially susceptible to such postmemory. As a result, when an Israeli perceives that they may be getting victimized – regardless of whether or not connected to the Holocaust – post-trauma symptoms may appear and prompt them to overreact as if the issue is somehow connected to the sensitive and intense event of the Holocaust.

While the nuances of Hirsch's research are worth an entire analysis in itself, the takeaway for this research is that this concept of *postmemory* is present in the past and current conflict between Arabs and Jews. Specifically, those who have lived through the harsher periods of Israel's road to sovereignty (namely, the Holocaust, the Six-Day War, and the more recent Lebanon Wars) actually pass their experiences onto the younger generations of their family, who have not been exposed to trauma. With their vivid descriptions of traumatic experiences and the indoctrination of contempt against Palestinians, the Jewish postmemory has actually fueled some of the infighting of the Israeli-Palestinian Conflict (Hirsch, 1997). As a result of this postmemory, Hirsch argued that Israelis have often been quick to react (and overreact) to hostility. Israeli Jews born in the 2010s may have not experienced trauma firsthand, but Hirsch argues that they may as well have been there during the Holocaust or the Six-Day War or the Lebanon wars.

Steir-Livny (2016) corroborated research that LaCapra and Hirsch conducted. Namely, he affirms the concepts of *acting out* and *postmemory* (LaCapra, 2001; Hirsch, 1997). Steir-Livny additionally asserts that, in conjunction with this past research, there remain similarities between the Holocaust (in which the Jews were the victims) and the current Israeli-Palestinian Conflict (in which Israelis share the responsibility of being perpetrators). Thus, there is a mixed responsibility in this conflict.

Certainly the negative impact of the Holocaust has been minimized (Steir-Livny, 2016). That is, some hold a somewhat pervasive idea that the victimization of the Jews during the Holocaust has been overblown. Consequently, Israelis try to emphasize the idea

82

that they were (and are still) eternal victims of anti-Semitic rhetoric and violence, feeling a need to "prove" that they have been on the receiving end of injustice.

Of course, even if some Palestinians hold that Jews were not as targeted during the Holocaust as is reported, history certainly affirms that the Jews were, in fact, brutally slaughtered and victimized. However, it is with this eschewal by Palestinians that many Israeli Defense Soldiers justify their harsh retaliations. While proponents of Israeli retaliation argue that the community has simply learned how to prevent a massacre like what they faced at the hands of the Nazis, critics of Israeli retaliation argue that the community has now achieved a shared cruelty with the Nazis (Steir-Livny, 2016).

Iliceto et al. (2011) felt that some of the research on trauma transmission was conflicting, and wanted to discover if vicarious trauma can be passed down the generational line. Presently, most research suggests that vicarious trauma can, indeed, be passed down at least a single generation. The researchers here, though, wanted to see if the grandchildren of Holocaust survivors experienced secondhand trauma. The researchers took 124 Holocaust survivors' grandchildren and had them complete the State-Trait Anger Expression Inventory to assess for anger, the TEMPS-A to evaluate temperament, the 9 Attachment Profile to assess for personality traits, and the Beck Hopelessness Scale to measure hopelessness. The researchers argue that their data does not support Hirsch and LaCapra's notion that the effects of trauma are actually passed down to the second generation. However, traits of anger, irritability, and negativity did seem to be passed down, including frustration directed at God. This suggests that while the trauma itself is not passed down, the negative impacts of trauma can, in fact, be passed down to a younger generation.

In the Israeli-Palestinian Conflict, many of the participants were born into an environment in which they were taught to distrust the other side (i.e., Jews distrust Arabs, Arabs mistrust Jews). Even if younger generations have not experienced trauma by the other side, the negative impressions they have of the other side may already be imprinted on them. Shapiro and Goldberg (2002) published several interviews they had conducted in Israel and Palestinian territory for their documentary, <u>Promises</u>. One Jewish child spoke of his daily experience of onboarding a public transit bus: "When I get on, I'm anxious, so I look for suspicious people. If I see a really scary person, I watch him. I try to get off before he does. I keep waiting for the explosion; I count the seconds." A statement like this came from a young Jewish boy *who has no history of trauma* and was made *during a time of peace* (i.e., before the fallout from the failure of the Camp David Summit). Another Palestinian child recounts, "I wanted to cut that soldier in half, shoot him, or blow him up to avenge [my brother]" who had been immediately executed when he threw rocks at the Israeli military. Despite having no personal experience with explosives, this child immediately resorted to thoughts of "blowing up" his adversary, which is an abnormally escalated response in comparison to other children around the world who would be more likely to resort to having desires of engaging in fisticuffs or stabbing as the ultimate conceptualization of violence (Merrick, Kandel, & Omar, 2013).

Ultimately, it is quite difficult to provide a term that encapsulates all of the phenomena just described in one fell swoop, and there is much complexity to the idea that the descendant of a PTSD sufferer can acquire PTSD-like symptoms despite having never personally dealt with trauma. The concept *is* similar in scope to complex trauma, but is different in the intensity of the manifestations of symptoms (i.e., complex trauma is to PTSD what dysthymia is to major depressive disorder). Other terms like "perpetual trauma," "trauma transference," "secondary trauma," or "vicarious intergenerational trauma" have been suggested. While there is no term that perfectly summates the complexity of this concept, the research that follows refers to this concept as Transgenerational Trauma Transmission (TTT).

Transgenerational Trauma Transmission

Origins of TTT

Perhaps the best layman's description of Transgenerational Trauma Transmission (TTT) was conveyed by the master of suspense Alfred Hitchcock, who famously declared, "There is no terror in the bang, only in the anticipation of it." It is not only the trauma itself that may be transmitted, but the *idea* that the trauma could happen again. The bequeathing of emotional trauma has been observed in both mankind and nature alike. Most recently, Dias and Ressler (2014) took several mice and simultaneously administered painful electrical shocks and acetophenone, a pleasant scent that is similar to the scent of cherries and almonds. Unsurprisingly, the mice learned to associate acetophenone with pain, and trembled whenever the scent was present, even when shocks were no longer being administered. Dias and Ressler (2014) subsequently had these conditioned mice produce offspring, and then had the offspring produce children of their own (i.e., a third generation). Despite having never been shocked themselves, both the second generation and third generation of mice shuddered when confronted with acetophenone, suggesting that the distress was genetically inherited from their parents and grandparents.

In application to the human race, Atkinson et al. (2014) described the phenomenon simply as trauma that is experienced by one group of people, and then re-experienced by generations that follow. Dudgeon et al. (2014) expanded upon this by saying that when a child experiences mental or emotional distress as a result of a parent's violent event, this specifically is TTT. Unsurprisingly, most previous attempts to understand TTT have occurred through the lens of the sting of the Holocaust (Braga, Mello, & Fiks, 2012; Kellerman, 2001; Hirsch, 2008).

Hirsch (2008), who is attributed with coming up with the concept of postmemory, describes second-generation Holocaust survivors as the "guardians of the Holocaust," those who keep alive the memory of the Shoah. Though these guardians of the Holocaust did not directly endure the genocide, the traumatic experiences of their parents were transferred down through different media. Braga, Mello, and Fiks (2012) explain that the Holocaust was not only the impetus for research on TTT, but that the Holocaust also has dominated all of the research on the topic as well. Psychiatrist Vivian Rakoff authored the first published article on the phenomenon in 1966 when she noticed an onslaught of "survivor syndrome" in the citizens of Montreal – a city in which thousands of Holocaust survivors settled after liberation (Braga et al., 2012). However, the survivor guilt that she observed was not only occurring in Holocaust survivors, but also their children. It was believed that studying this phenomenon would not only help the individuals affected by it, but also help to understand the Holocaust as a whole.

Rakoff noted that the symptoms of TTT included "distrust of the world, impaired parental function, chronic sorrow, inability to communicate feelings, an ever-present fear of danger, pressure for educational achievement, separation anxiety, lack of entitlement, unclear boundaries, and overprotectiveness within a narcissist family system" (Braga et al., 2012, p. 2). Rakoff observed that Montreal teenagers who were the offspring of Holocaust survivors showed signs of mental disturbances that were atypical from their peers. Yet, these observations only instigated modest investigations into the matter. Further, studies were beleaguered by a lack of control groups and a lack of standardized instruments to assess the phenomenon, and findings could not be generalized as evidence was largely subjective rather than empirical – limitations that plague most research on TTT even today. While several case studies have indicated TTT, none of them were systematic in nature and therefore have been unable to pinpoint the manifestation of TTT in children. As a result, the findings on the topic have been inconclusive. Today, the youngest Holocaust survivors are septuagenarians; in other words, time is running out to study the relationship between TTT and the Holocaust.

Kellerman (2001) defined TTT as the "transmission of psychological trauma across generational lines" (p. 36) and that a child's absorption of emotional scars from a Holocaust-surviving parent is largely unavoidable. As such, understanding this concept is important, not only from a psychological angle, but also a legal one: insurance companies would need to consider its implications for consumers, while international criminal courts could indict perpetrators of trauma and genocide for inflicting harm on *multiple* generations.

Hirsch (2008) explored different tropes that capture the trauma of the Holocaust, most notably photographs. These photographs need not capture acts of terror in order to invoke trauma, but rather, a burned shoe or a mutilated teddy bear are enough to potentially transfer the trauma to the next person. Images of the actual perpetrators and/or victims also have an innate ability to capture the transgressions, even if no violence is displayed in the photo itself. Hirsch concludes the severest of tropes are the ones that capture the essence of maternal loss: it is inherently bothersome to imagine one's mother going through such atrocities, and any loss felt by the mother has the capability of being vicariously felt by her children.

That being said, proximity to individuals who suffered trauma is not enough to "diagnose" TTT. McNally (2014) studied TTT in Northern Ireland by conducting semi-structured interviews with three male and four female ($N = 7$) Irish Christians (a mix of Catholic and Protestant Christians), all of whom had experienced the loss of a young member of their immediate family. McNally (2014) concluded that it is improper to automatically attribute TTT to a distressed individual just because they have relational proximity to an individual who suffered an initial trauma. Rather, Duran and Duran (1995) characterized TTT as being a type of historical trauma that has embedded in a culture so deeply that the trauma is normal for that particular culture. Many cultures support the notion of *lay trauma theory,* which posits that trauma is a natural (i.e., unpreventable) phenomenon and therefore, post-trauma should be expected (Alexander et al., 2004).

Operationalization of Transgenerational Trauma Transmission

As of publication, diagnostic criteria for TTT cannot be found in the DSM, ICD, or any clinical manual. For all intents and purposes, it is still an undefined, nebulous concept that does not have an agreed-upon operational definition. In the spirit of DSM and ICD diagnoses, and based on the literature that is available regarding TTT, I am presenting a fluid operational definition for the purpose of this study.

Transgenerational Trauma Transmission can be described with the following criteria:

A. A member of the person's immediate family (i.e., parent, grandparent, sibling) has been exposed to a traumatic event that involved potential death or potential injury, and later recounted the event with inclusion of these details:
    a. The offender's perceived race or religion
    b. The setting (e.g., bus stop, shopping mall, house of worship, etc.)
    c. The perceived meaning of the encounter
B. After the recounting of the traumatic event(s), the person experienced some of the following:
    a. Cautiousness or avoidance of the perceived race or religion of the offender
    b. Avoidance of the setting
    c. Persistent thoughts about the event that did not happen to them

Indications of Transgenerational Trauma Transmission

Denham (2008) notes that a difference exists between *trauma* and *trauma response*; it is not the event itself that causes distress, but the way the event is processed. In that vein, Braga et al. (2012) echoed Hirsch's emphasis on *themes* rather than specific details: at its most technical, TTT is not necessarily the passing down of trauma itself, but the passing down of its experiential themes. Despite having the word "trauma" in its name, TTT is not confirmed to the extent that it necessarily results in psychopathology. Kellerman (2001) noted that only one-third of the studies he reviewed indicated significant psychopathological differences between those exposed to TTT and that of control groups. While TTT can be confirmed as a phenomenon that appears to increase susceptibility to trauma, it is too early to cite it as psychopathological as it does not result in mental disorders, but rather personality deficits. To that end, it must be emphasized that TTT is *not* Complex PTSD (CPTSD), a concept coined by Herman (2012) who described CPTSD as a trauma that manifests as a consequence of prolonged neglect and/or abuse. CPTSD is often perpetrated by one or two individuals, whereas TTT is often perpetrated by multiple individuals and is processed differently than CPTSD.

However, that is not to say that TTT has never been linked to forms of PTSD. Yehuda et al. (1998) found that children who had parents suffering from post-trauma symptoms tended to also develop post-trauma symptoms themselves, and Solomon et al. (1988) linked soldiers with TTT as being more susceptible to PTSD. Still, Kellerman (2001) notes that in the past, TTT has been treated as if a "lesser-form of PTSD," when in reality, TTT is a completely different manifestation of post-traumatic effects. In fact, a counter-argument against the nefarious nature of TTT is that the Holocaust has also positively improved the lives of many survivors' offspring by making an otherwise-horrific event more meaningful, while also increasing peoples' compassion for human suffering (Denham, 2008). If there is TTT, then there also likely exists "transgenerational growth transmission," akin to there existing a post-traumatic growth as a counterpart to PTSD (Tedeschi & Calhoun, 2009).

The notion that TTT could have a positive impact was echoed by Braga et al. (2012) when they observed that children were much more likely to overcome trauma if their parents were first able to do so. This finding also corroborates themes Denham (2008) found in an earlier study that indicate TTT had produced significant resiliency in the Couer d'Alene Native Americans in Northern Idaho, as well as descendants of the survivors of the Holocaust.

Conversely, many of the early studies of TTT indicated that children who eventually suffer TTT often experience it at the same age their parents endured trauma (Kellerman, 2001). Kellerman describes TTT as manifesting in either a "direct and specific" way (i.e., children suffer from the same symptoms as the adult), or in an "indirect and general" way in which the parent is unable to care well for the child, which leads to general dysfunction.

Finally, Kellerman (2001) established seven specific risk factors for TTT. Individuals were more likely to be negatively affected by TTT when they were characterized as: (a) offspring who were born shortly after a trauma experienced by their parents, (b) an only-child or first-born child, (c) children whose set of parents *both* endured the same trauma, (d) children who were born after their parents had previously lost a child (i.e., "replacement children"), (e) offspring of parents who had endured "extraordinary mental suffering and significant loss" (p. 43), (f) children who were engaged in an enmeshed relationship with their parent(s), or (g) children who were raised in a household in which past trauma was talked about either too much or too little. Braga et al. (2012) added that those who coped healthily with TTT frequently used humor, whereas individuals who did not like to speak of the trauma or preferred to keep the trauma secret most often displayed negative symptoms.

Transgenerational Trauma Transmission in the Israeli-Palestinian Conflict

Denham (2008) described TTT as having the potential to actually result in healthy coping. Specifically, the telling and re-telling of traumatic events can have positive effects if three specific criteria are met regarding the individual telling the story: (1) the story helps to create meaning, (2) the story helps the individual to achieve control and order, and (3) the story helps to provide perspective about current events. For most Jews – whether they be modern-day Israelis or Holocaust survivors – these components are arguably achieved.

The effects of TTT are not limited to Holocaust survivors (Kellerman, 2001). Leiken (2005) wrote the groundbreaking article "Europe's Angry Muslims," which examined the recurring phenomena that most acts of terrorism are committed by second-generation immigrants who are displeased with their host country. In terms of the Israeli-Palestinian Conflict, much of the demographic of Israel falls under this category of being second-generation immigrants, making the land a ripe target for contemporary terrorism by those affected by TTT.

In a study that occurred in the Gaza Strip during the Second Intifada, Thabet, Abed, and Vostanis (2001) investigated the prevalence of post-trauma stress reactions in 286 Palestinian children by using the Gaza Traumatic Events Checklist, the Impact of Event Scale, and the General Health Questionnaire. At that time, children in Gaza experienced an average of four traumatic events, and one-third of the children reported post-trauma stress reactions. In another study, children between the ages of 10 and 18 were randomly selected throughout the Gaza Strip to complete the Checklist of Traumatic Experiences, the Personality Assessment Questionnaire, and the Symptoms of PTSD Scale (Altawil et al., 2008). Altawil et al. discovered that every child – without exception – had been exposed to at least three trauma-inducing events. 97% of the participants had been exposed to the sounds of explosions and 84% had personally witnessed artillery shelling. 41% of the participants appeared to suffer from some form of PTSD.

Finally, the question must be asked: if this phenomenon truly exists, then why has there not been more research on the topic? I have come up with two potential reasons why this might be the case. The first is that TTT may ultimately be something that is viewed as unpreventable, which would instigate many cultures to simply accept the phenomenon as a fact of life as is done with other unpreventable phenomena, like sudden illness or natural disasters. More importantly, locations where TTT can be measured seem to manifest in locations in which protracted social conflict is present. In other words, it can be exceptionally dangerous to attempt to study this concept: it appears that to get the best data to increase validity on the subject, one must sacrifice some safety in turn.

Summary

For too long, trauma has been understood through the simplistic lens of PTSD. For Israelis and Palestinians who have not migrated out of their trauma environments, PTSD is largely irrelevant, paving the way for CTS as a main mode of understanding the way trauma manifests in this Middle Eastern region. However, even CTS is limited in terms of this specific Israeli-Palestinian Conflict, which is a 3000 year-old conflict that is just one chapter (albeit a large one) within the Arab-Israeli Conflict. For this reason, the concept of Transgenerational Trauma Transmission – which implies CTS as a component as it takes place over multiple generations – is the lens that this conflict's trauma was viewed through. This included consideration of the religious/eschatological realities of the Abrahamic religions, which is currently lacking in the literature.

Chapter 3: Research Design and Method

Chapter Overview

The manifestation of trauma within Israeli and Palestinian participants was studied in hopes of better understanding the etiology of Transgenerational Trauma Transmission (TTT). Due to the restrictive nature of DSM and ICD criteria, labels of trauma-based conditions (such as PTSD) were eschewed, and trauma was instead understood in the contexts they were presented by participants. The following research questions and research design have been crafted to best reflect the contextual background of each participant. The purpose of this chapter will be to establish the assessment instruments and procedures to be used in this study. A meta-analysis of potential ethical and validity issues is provided.

Research Design

The purpose of this study was to explore the manifestation of an understudied phenomenon (i.e., TTT) in the Israeli-Palestinian Conflict, prompting this research to be a clear example of a phenomenological qualitative exploratory study (Creswell, 2014). Phenomenological studies are interested in the experiences of individuals (Smith, Flowers, & Larkin, 2009) and seek to answer the question, "What is it like to be human?," or in the scope of this particular study, "What is it like to be an Israeli/Palestinian living in Israel/Palestine?"

When examining phenomenology, there is a need to be hyper-conscious of personal perceptions, one's own natural attitudes about objects, and to be aware of one's own biased reflexes (Smith et al., 2009). In terms of this study, there is perhaps no better example of this than the western reflex that "trauma" is automatically synonymous with "PTSD" despite the fact that the clinical definition of PTSD does not distinguish between different manifestations of post-traumatic responses (Wamser-Nanney & Vandenberg, 2013; Tennant, 2004; Haj, 2015; Geist, 2012). This misnomer plays an important role in the premise of the need for research on TTT.

Phenomenological research is presented with the philosophy that the world itself is external: there is the world, and then there are those who are in that world. Smith et al. (2009) explain the reason for this is because "our sense of self is holistic and is engaged in looking at the world, rather than being subsumed with it" (p. 18). Whereas most approaches view the individual person as an object within the world, the phenomenological approach views the bodily self as a tool for interaction with the world: people have individual bodies, therefore people cannot fully experience another's reality. Instead, the attempt is to try to understand the phenomena that comprise another's world by getting as close as one can to experiencing their reality.

While the primary design for this exploratory study is phenomenological, aspects of narrative and ethnographic designs were also incorporated. There are specific reasons as to why these are appropriate additions to this study, and it is important to discuss exactly what this acute combination of methodology offers that other approaches do not. In particular, it can be argued that a purely phenomenological approach would have been more appropriate than a hybrid design that also incorporates narrative design and ethnography, but there are specific reasons why this notion is not accurate.

On the surface, a pure phenomenological approach does seem like the most logical approach for this study as its purpose was to explore the implications of an understudied phenomenon. However, an emphasis on the meaning-making processes would be lost, as etymology would become the focus instead. Especially in terms of the Israeli-Palestinian Conflict, the meaning-making process is much more important than trying to add a fresh observation in regard to its origins, which has been attempted *ad nauseam*.

Further, Stevens (2007) has described international psychology as an alternative psychology. Mainstream psychology suggests that any cognitive process can be empirically measured, while alternative psychology emphasizes the value of meaning-making within the cultural context the phenomenon is found. Mainstream psychology tries to understand the "why" of an issue; alternative psychology focuses on the "how." In regards to the Israeli-Palestinian Conflict, the "why" has already been answered; the crux of the conflict lies in understanding the "how." Further, the analysis of TTT in this study is not intended to only study the phenomenon itself, but also to study the impact that the phenomenon has had on Middle Eastern culture. As a result, the narrative design was nearly as crucial as the phenomenological.

Narrative studies are most useful when thematic elements are being explored, and further, when the data collection technique will include interviews that largely consist of storytelling (Creswell, 2014). Normally, narrative studies are conducted with a smaller sample size; the quality of discussion is favored over the quantity of discussions (Kim, 2016). This study had 17 participants; therefore, the emphasis was clearly put on the quality of discussions rather than the quantity.

Narrative research was intended as a marriage between scientific research and qualitative exploration, and was originally birthed as a break from the assumption that empirical science is the only source of knowledge; previous to narrative studies, human pursuits of knowledge that used non-empirical methods were considered a pseudoscience (Kim, 2016). Conversely, narrative design assumes that scientific knowledge can be achieved not only through the natural sciences, but also political discourse.

Psychological processes are not cut-and-dry; humans experience uncertainty and complexity, instability and uniqueness. When one accepts this, there are two ways to view the world: paradigmatically and narratively. The former is "formal and empirical" and the latter creates "lifelike" stories, but both complement each other (Kim, 2016, p. 10). In the past, the emphasis has clearly been put on the paradigmatic model, but this rigidity poses a risk of ignoring the important meaning-making processes that humans possess.

It is crucial to accept that there is no method to perfectly capture the Israeli or Palestinian experience without actually being Israeli or Palestinian – not even the most rigorous natural science can achieve this (Kim, 2016). A phenomenological design alone would overlook this important aspect, and therefore, the narrative design was incorporated to ensure that binary thinking is not being utilized in light of the major cultural differences between Israelis, Palestinians, and neutral observers.

In this same line of thinking, the purpose of ethnography is to tell a story that is "credible, rigorous, and authentic" (Fetterman, 2010, p. 1), and is the preferred design when studying a particular cultural group, especially those whose voice has gone under-represented in the context of their own indigenous culture (Creswell, 2014). An open mind is particularly crucial in ethnographic design as this allows for the researcher to tap into sources of data that were not anticipated when formulating the initial research design. This is partially due to the fact that ethnographic research is based on the relativist perspective, meaning that many cultures have phenomena occurring that do not fit into other countries' schemas (Fontaine, 2011). In this case, the focus remains on trauma as understood in Israeli and Palestinian contexts, which is not necessarily congruent with the understanding of trauma in the western world. Combining the need for qualitative narrative interviews and the focus on these two cultural groups, there is a clear necessity to incorporate both narrative design and ethnography in addition to the basic phenomenological design.

It should be noted that an assumption of ethnographic study is that the researcher be immersed in the culture he/she is studying. As a result of this assumption, I traveled to Israel and spent a week in the culture to understand it better before actually carrying out research. Without this component, a case study design might have been a more appropriate methodology choice, but because the study is intended to be indicative of the Israeli-Palestinian culture at large and specifically aimed to make a statement about Israelis and Palestinians in general, an ethnographic mindset was embraced.

In 2003, American student Rachel Corrie submerged herself into the Israeli-Palestinian Conflict, living in Palestine amidst intense infighting between the Israelis and Palestinians. In an email to her mother, Corrie stated, "No amount of reading, attendance at conferences, documentary viewing, and word of mouth could have prepared me for the reality of the situation here. You just can't imagine it unless you see it" (Omeish & Omeish, 2006). Shortly after she sent this email, Corrie was killed by an Israeli soldier who bulldozed her, putting the exclamation mark on her proclamation that the long and complicated Israeli-Palestinian Conflict is something that is best experienced, not read about.

Research Questions

Research Question 1: How does Transgenerational Trauma Transmission (TTT) manifest in Israeli and Palestinian young adults?

Research Question 2: How does religious identity affect the lenses of Israelis and Palestinians in conflict?

Population and Sample

A homogenous purposive sample was selected for this study: all participants were those affected (directly or indirectly) by the Israeli-Palestinian Conflict and self-identified as either Israeli or Palestinian. The study ultimately collected data from 17 participants, which is an adequate sample size for a study focused on narrative stories; narrative studies generally only have one or two participants (Creswell, 2013). Even still, the smaller sample size compromises external validity, but, again, this is not a massive problem as generalizability was not the grand purpose of this study.

Setting

It is ideal to interview participants in their most natural setting (Creswell, 2014). In this instance, that setting is the nation of Israel and the Palestinian territories. While this study could feasibly be converted as a cross-cultural study involving Israeli-American or Palestinian-American immigrants, a study in this setting would run a much higher risk of westernization influence and acculturation biases. Therefore, all interviews were conducted in Israel and Palestine. Participants were interviewed at a location of their choice to make them most comfortable. Two Palestinians requested a private setting in their own home to ensure comfort, privacy, and confidentiality.

Procedure

As the researcher, I needed collaboration with an on-ground agency in Israel/Palestine to recruit participants, and the participants needed to be native to the Middle East. Participants needed to be able to speak English as I am monolingual. On average, each interview took about an hour per participant.

The interview was usually conducted over a meal that was provided by the researcher. The participant was explained the basics of the research purpose, but was not immediately told that the study was specifically looking at trauma. Instead, they were informed that the broad purpose of the study was to study the effects of conflict on the individual and family dynamics. Participants gave verbal informed consent that they understood the purpose of the research and that they were not being coerced to comply with the study. Oral informed consent was preferred over written informed consent for the aforementioned emphasis on confidentiality; having a written document with the name and signature of a participant can potentially compromise the safety of the participant as all documents entering and leaving Israel and Palestine are subject to seizure (and, in fact, were seized when I first entered the country).

The participants were given a loose interview in which handwritten notes were taken. The nature of the questions was sensitive, especially in a culture where one cannot be sure who is friend or foe. As such, no recording devices were used. It must be reiterated that outside researchers are not trusted in studies dealing with trauma (Straker, 2013), and that those on the "outside" of ethnic issues are often distrusted by those on the "inside" (Hugman et al., 2011). The use of a recording device may have had the impact to change participant responses and behavior as there exists a natural cognizance by participants that they are being observed. This is known as the Hawthorne Effect (Cone & Foster, 2006), and it could result in a participant embellishing a story or conversely withholding information if they are mindful that they are being recorded outright. For this reason, handwritten notes were used in place of audio and visual recording devices. Even audio recordings – which are much less intrusive than visual recordings – still pose a risk of influencing participants' responses and pose a risk of identifying information accidentally being obtained by someone other than the one who is intended to have the data. While this may only be considered a minimal risk if the study were conducted elsewhere, the risk is magnified in Israel and Palestine, where a person's identity can pose a serious threat to their safety (Zilkha, 1992).

Upon completion of the interview, each participant was debriefed. This included an explanation that the researcher was most interested in the manifestation of trauma and the religious impact of participants in the Israeli-Palestinian Conflict. Each participant was offered a referral to a therapist in Israel/Palestine if they felt they needed to further sort through the topics that were stirred up in the interview. I agreed to pay for the first session with this therapist, but none of the participants took advantage of this offer.

Validity

The level of external validity was contingent on the sample actually being representative of the greater population (Creswell, 2013). External validity is at its strongest when using randomized sampling, but due to the nature and limited availability of participants, nonrandom purposive sampling was required. The sensitive nature of this study prevented random sampling from being used, but increasing the sample size in potential future studies also could increase external validity.

However, the aim of this study was not generalizability. Instead, internal validity was favored over external validity for this particular endeavor as the exploration was based on whether or not symptoms of TTT can be attributed to the hostile environment alone, or if there were other factors at play. Therefore, it would increase internal validity by minimizing the potential of outside variables that might help explain the phenomenon. Nonrandom purposive sampling helps in that approach as the focus remains on the specific set of participants who all have the common thread of involvement (direct or indirect) in the Israeli-Palestinian Conflict. Further, internal validity would be increased as a single researcher was the one conducting all interviews.

One threat to internal validity is the time that has taken place between recounted events. For instance, if an adult has experienced combat several decades ago, the fact that it occurred so long ago could mean that the adult has already worked through these issues. To that end, participants may have also processed symptoms of TTT so long ago that they may not even be aware of any lingering effects from it, or they may have already made a conscious decision to manage or even reject the symptoms.

Another threat to internal validity is if the questions used in the interviews do not actually measure the concept of TTT, or more pointedly, if TTT could feasibly be explained by other phenomena (Creswell, 2014). In that vein, self-report is also a threat to internal validity as response bias may influence participants' answers (Van de Mortel, 2008). In these instances, exaggeration may occur if the participant sees a benefit in engaging in it.

This is profoundly more significant in terms of the Israeli-Palestinian Conflict, in which participants may feel the need to justify their experiences, actions, and beliefs in light of knowing that their political opponents are also being interviewed and assumedly justifying their worldview. This can be minimized by assuring participants that neither they (nor the population they represent) will benefit from placing blame on any party, as culpability for the conflict is not relevant to this research.

Instrumentation

All participants were asked a set of qualitative questions to answer both research questions, and these interviews were administered by the researcher. Specifically, every participant's gender and age were taken, and then each one was asked the following set of seven questions:

- Where did you grow up?
- What was your family's religion when you were growing up?
- What would you classify yourself as now?
- What do you remember your parents telling you about (Muslims/Jews)?
- Are you familiar with the (Jewish/Muslim) prophecy regarding Gog and Magog?
- Can you describe a traumatic experience you've had?
- Can you describe a traumatic experience one of your parents had with (Muslims/Jews)?

As time permitted and the direction of the interview permitted, I asked additional questions, which were pulled from a more extensive set of questions. The full set of questions can be found in Appendix A.

Recognition theory drove some of the development of the interviews. Friedman (2016) argued that there are gaps of formal recognition between the participants of the Israeli-Palestinian Conflict. Specifically, recognition of the other as a nation and recognition of the other's sovereignty as a state are lacking. In a case study that examines the governments from 1969 to 1973 (Meir Government), 1993 to 1995 (Second Rabin Government), and 2009 to 2012 (Second Netanyahu Government), recognition theory was proposed as a means to delineate the actual conflict in the Israeli-Palestinian Conflict. That is, if both sides could even partially recognize that the other has fulfilled the conditions of statehood (i.e., either recognizing its peoplehood or its statehood), then the Israeli-Palestinian Conflict may not be as exacerbated as it has been throughout history. For this reason, some questions within the survey were focused on helping participants attain this recognition.

The question arises why a time-tested trauma questionnaire would not be used, and the reason is because no questionnaires have been culturally validated in Israel or Palestine. Israel as a nation is young; so are its psychological programs. The Israeli Psychological Association (IPA), which is the Israeli equivalent to the American Psychological Association, was only developed in 1957, and the Israeli title of "psychologist" (and the regulations that govern the field) were not formed until 1977 (Welfel & Khamush, 2012). The IPA has not developed any trauma questionnaires that are specific to Israeli and/or Palestinian contexts, and outside of Israel, there are currently no instruments that have been developed to gauge levels of transgenerational transmission, nor has any instrument that assesses trauma been culturally validated in cross-cultural situations (Mollica et al., 1992). As such, the difficult task of developing an instrument that would not only assess this phenomenon, but would also be sufficiently culturally valid, was posed. To do so, the Harvard Trauma Questionnaire was used as a guide.

The Harvard Trauma Questionnaire (HTQ) is a trauma questionnaire that was developed for use with refugees in cross-cultural settings (Mollica et al., 1992). Currently, the HTQ is valued as a culturally-relevant trauma assessment tool that is used across the world – as far west as the United States and as far east as the Philippines: the Torture Abolition and Survivors Coalition (TASSC) in Washington, D.C. uses it in psychotherapy with those seeking asylum and the Balay Rehabilitation Center in Manila uses it to support their mission of providing psychosocial services to refugees, displaced persons, and torture survivors. Nine of the questions that were developed for this study were directly adapted from the Harvard Trauma Questionnaire, specifically:

- Do you sometimes feel that the events your loved ones faced are going to happen to you?
- Do you avoid putting yourself in situations in which the trauma that happened to your loved ones could happen to you?
- Do you have recurring nightmares of events that have not actually happened to you in real life?
- What sort of events or situations trigger these "memories" or thoughts?
- Do you find yourself more irritable after you think about these things?
- Do you struggle to express to others your feelings about these events?
- Do you feel guilty for not having personally experienced these events that your loved ones have?
- When you look at an (Muslim/Jew), do you assume they mean peace or harm towards you?
- Do you feel betrayed by people who have not actually personally betrayed you?

One of the questions in the interview asked a hypothetical question: "what would you like to say to your enemies" if given the chance? Lewis (2016) told the story of Israeli psychologists Kahneman and Tvserky, two secular Jews who studied the way the human mind systematically creates an alternative reality in the face of distress, referred to as the "Undoing Project." Imagining these alternative realities – the world of the "couldashouldawoulda" – helps people who experienced trauma to "undo" the trauma by re-living what they "should" have done in traumatic situations. Lewis concluded from these Israeli studies that when people make decisions (whether in the face of trauma or not), the goal is not to maximize happiness, but actually to simply minimize regret. The question "what would you like to say to your enemies" was designed to give participants an opportunity to consider this alternative reality.

Data Processing

In quantitative research, objective instruments make it possible to draw out data, but in qualitative research, this responsibility falls on the researcher during the actual interview. In fact, in a qualitative exploratory study, the researcher is the key instrument as he/she conducts the interview (Creswell, 2014). Therefore, after data collection, thematic analysis was conducted with Computer Assisted Qualitative Data Analysis Software – specifically, NVivo. Qualitative researchers generally use both an inductive and deductive process (Creswell, 2014). The researcher is constantly using an inductive reasoning to identify emerging themes, while he/she then uses deduction to find more evidence that speaks to the themes that have emerged. As such, the direction of a qualitative study cannot be fully known until after the data collection process has concluded. Arriving at the data collection process with the findings already assumed has great potential to detract from the validity of the study (Creswell, 2013). With this in mind, the following analysis followed a basic three-step plan: use induction during data collection, use NVivo on the notes collected to help discover what themes have emerged, and use deduction to draw conclusions.

It is also important for any qualitative study to consider the participants' meaning-making process. The way a participant will respond to the interviews cannot be anticipated, and again, attempting to do so leads to bias. Bearing this in mind, Hugman et al. (2011) developed a participatory action model in which participants are encouraged to take ownership of their role in the study. There is an ancient Confucian adage that speaks to the idea that if one tells someone something, they will forget; if one shows them, they may remember; but if one involves them, they will learn (Kuang, 2016).

The participatory action model additionally requires an extra layer of ethical accountability as participants have a say in the end result of the study. Specifically for this study, the meaningful themes described by the participants during interviews guided the data processing and discussion, which results in a true emergent design. That is, the design emerged out of the methodology rather than the other way around (Creswell, 2014). Ideally, this leads to a more holistic understanding of TTT: the general idea has already been described, but some important themes related to TTT (including religious interplay) may emerge. The participatory action model is further discussed in the ethical assurances ahead.

Assumptions

There is a strong precedent for participants of protracted social conflicts to initially distrust outside primary investigators. Straker (2013) cited Continuous Traumatic Stress as a frequent byproduct in which sufferers do not trust ethnic outsiders. In such conflicts, even one's neighbor may be a member of the opposite political camp, making it very difficult to truly trust anyone outside of one's own household. As a result, outside therapists and researchers are often clumped into this category of people who are not deemed trustworthy. It was assumed that this distrust would be extended to me as the researcher, but that those who got past this concern and did choose to participate in the study were honest throughout the process of data collection and that they believed the study was being conducted in good faith (i.e., not trying to prove a political point). It was assumed that all participants would be familiar with the western concept of trauma and at least be familiar with the historical narrative of the Holocaust. It was assumed that every participant had been directly or indirectly impacted by the Israeli-Palestinian Conflict. It was assumed that the assurance of confidentiality would not result in participants lying or embellishing their accounts. It was assumed that participants had not been coerced to take part in this study, and that the sample was representative of the population they had been drawn from. It was assumed that participants had not acculturated outside of their native culture, which is important because those who have not acculturated to other cultures are more likely to strongly identify with their native identity (Fail, Thompson, & Walker, 2004).

104

Ethical Assurances

Participatory Action Model

Hugman et al. (2011) emphasized that all researchers need accountability, and that the ends of a research project do not justify the means. This research project espouses this mindset and recognizes that deceptive and/or unethical actions not only hurt the research project at hand, but also the field in the long run. Pittaway described a personal experience in which he had a group of female participants who had previously been manipulated by researchers and treated purely as "data" rather than human beings. Upon Pittaway's introduction, these previously-exploited participants expressed hesitancy to assist in his project. However, because they had previously known Pittaway personally, they reluctantly agreed to participate in the research. Pittaway used this as an opportunity to empower his participants to become advocates for other women within their communities. Pittaway named this community-oriented method the participatory action model, defined as when participants become part of the solution (Hugman et al., 2011).

Treating participants as "data" has long-term consequences and neglects this model. The research presented here espoused the participatory action model whenever possible, which not only stimulated participants' interest in the study, but is also ethically responsible.

Practical Actions

No participants were forced into participating in this study, and all answers during the interview and survey process were given voluntarily. Each of the participants gave oral consent after being provided a recruitment flyer that was approved by the Institutional Review Board (IRB). The flyer presented the potential dangers and risks associated with the study and outlined its scope. Participants were promised that data collected would remain confidential, that no audio or visual media was being used to record any aspect of the interviews, and that all raw data from the study would be kept in a secure location and then destroyed four years after the interview.

Recounting traumatic events can incite bad memories or prompt a person to relive the trauma (White, 1998). For this reason, the interviews could be stopped at any point at the request of the participant, and a local mental health professional was available within 24 hours to see the participant if necessary. Regardless of the participants' comfort with the questions, each one was presented contact information to an on-ground mental health agency that could provide long-term treatment. Participants were explained that they could rescind their involvement in the study at any time, up to the time of study publication.

Hugman et al. (2011) mentioned that researchers should be weary of providing high-value gifts to participants. For instance, providing money outright is discouraged as this can result in some ethical questions and impact the validity of the research. However, taking participants out to dinner or lunch is an acceptable way of rewarding participants, and is a gift that is most often cheerfully received by participants. Based on this counsel, I provided one meal for every participant during the actual interview. This remains an ethically-responsible gift for participants and helps maintain the validity of the experiment. Participants were given a free meal with the researcher, even if they ultimately decided during the meal to disallow their data from being included in the research.

All of the aforementioned techniques and ethical assurances were approved by the IRB (IRB #17-12-0027). The potential benefits of this study included adding to the present body of knowledge about trauma, understanding a previously understudied phenomenon (i.e., TTT), and contributing data to the literature on theories of non-western trauma. The participants were benefited by being given a tangible meal as well as by having their stories told (which would ideally produce feelings of empowerment and recognition).

Summary

Participants who identified as Palestinian and/or Israeli were interviewed with the intent to uncover symptoms of TTT, a previously unstudied phenomenon that seemed to be present in countries in perpetual conflict. Participants were assessed using interview questions and a survey created uniquely for the purposes of this study.

Expressions of particular themes were extracted and analyzed. A qualitative design with a focus on phenomenology was created to emphasize the exploratory nature of the data, allowing for an analysis that could account for thematic elements. The primary design of the study was phenomenological, which emphasized the epistemological assumption that research should be able to adequately understand a phenomenon. Meanwhile, aspects of both narrative design and ethnographic design were included to accentuate the ontological assumption that varying types of research can help best capture participants' realities (Creswell, 2013). The following chapter reports the results of this study.

Chapter 4: Results of the Study

Chapter Overview

From October 2018 to November 2018, I interviewed 17 participants for this study. The following chapter reflects the demographics of the participants, the setting in which they were interviewed, the procedure used during data collection, the techniques used in data analysis (including coding and thematic analysis), and the seven thematic conclusions that were drawn from this analysis. Additionally, a revised clinical operationalization of Transgenerational Trauma Transmission (TTT) was offered.

Findings

Demographics

Ten Israelis and seven Palestinians ($N = 17$) between the ages of 18 and 35 participated in this study (see Table 4). Of the participants, 11 were male (64.7%) and six were female (35.3%). Nine of the Israeli participants (52.9%) came from Jewish families, while one Israeli participant (5.9%) came from an anti-religious family; six of the Palestinian participants (35.2%) came from Muslim families, while one Palestinian participant (5.9%) came from a Christian family (see Diagram 1). However, eight of the participants (47.1%) (4 Israelis, 4 Palestinians) claimed to be unconcerned about religion in general and three of the participants (17.6%) (1 Israeli, 2 Palestinians) were conflicted about religion or expressed indecision about what religion they claim to be. Only three of the Israeli participants (17.6%) self-identified as religiously Jewish and only one (5.9%) of the Palestinian participants self-identified as Muslim, while two of the participants (11.8%) (both Israelis) expressed extreme distaste towards religion and a disbelief in God (see Diagram 2).

DIAGRAM 1: Family Religion

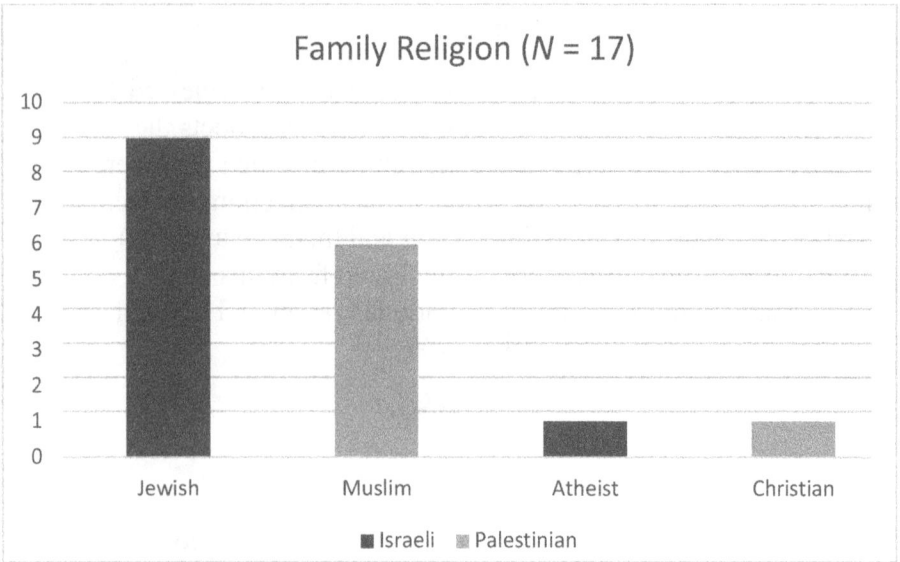

Family Religion (*N* = 17)

DIAGRAM 2: Personal Religion

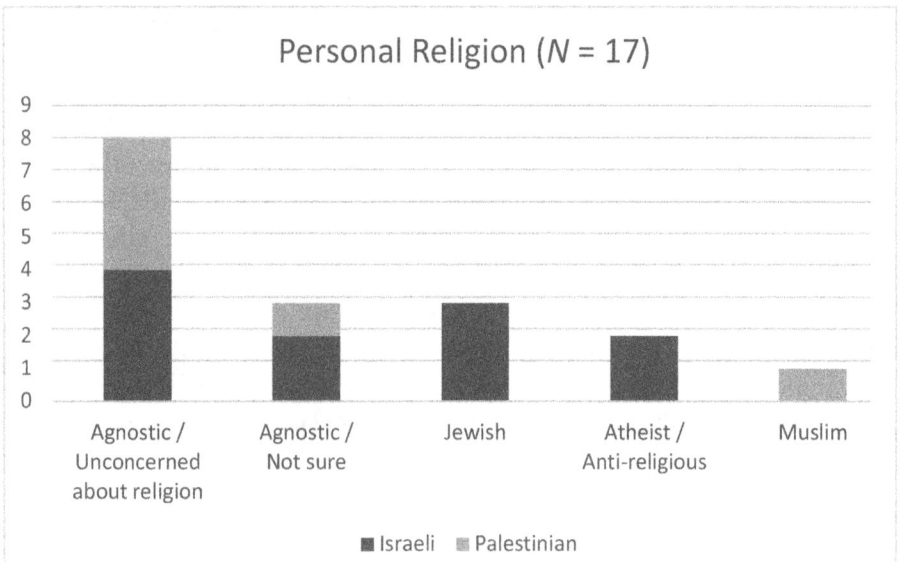

Personal Religion (*N* = 17)

TABLE 4: Demographics of Participants

Participant	Sex	Age	Location Raised	Family Religion	Personal Religion	Reported Trauma
P-1	M	23	Bethlehem	Muslim	Secular	No
P-2	M	19	Bethlehem	Muslim	Secular	No
P-3	F	19	Ramallah	Muslim	Muslim	Yes
P-4	M	21	Ramallah	Muslim	Secular	No
P-5	M	19	Jericho	Muslim	Secular	No
P-6	F	28	Bethlehem	Christian	Secular	Yes
P-7	M	23	Jericho	Muslim	Secular	No
I-1	F	29	Settlement	Ortho-Jew	Agnostic	No
I-2	M	32	Bethlehem	Ortho-Jew	Agnostic	No
I-3	M	25	Jerusalem	Jewish	Secular	No
I-4	F	30	Jerusalem	Ortho-Jew	Atheist	No
I-5	F	29	Settlement	Ortho-Jew	Modern-Orthodox	No
I-6	M	25	"Rural" Israel	Jewish	Secular	No
I-7	M	26	Otef Aza	Ortho-Jew	Secular	Yes
I-8	M	34	Tel Aviv	Jewish	Jewish	Yes – extreme PTSD
I-9	F	29	Jerusalem	Jewish	Modern-Jew	Yes (indirect only)
I-10	M	25	Amatz	anti-Jew	Secular	Yes

Setting

The political climate of Israel and Palestine is always tense, and my time there was no exception. I was never in (or near) precarious situations, but there were a few violent encounters between Israelis and Palestinians, including Palestinians shooting rockets into Israel and IDF responding by killing several Palestinians (Al-Jazeera, 2018; BBC News, 2018). When talking to my participants, I had to remain sensitive to the fact that I was discussing an ongoing conflict that directly affected them and their families.

110

Procedure

When I arrived in Israel, I communicated with my Israeli contact who had agreed to reach out to his students to see who would be willing to have a conversation with me. Unfortunately, this contact had gone on a business trip and had forgotten that I was coming at all, which I had not reminded him of immediately prior to my departure. I reached out to several universities (either by emailing them or by walking onto their campus and asking to speak with one of the program directors) to see if they could instead help me gather participants (whether Israeli or Palestinian). Hebrew Union College, the Jewish Institute of Religion, Tel Aviv University, Bethlehem University, Hebrew University, Rothberg International School, Jerusalem University College, Bethlehem Bible College, Al-Quds University (Old City Campus), and Birzeit University all either did not respond (if contact was made by email) or declined to reach out to students with my recruitment flyer (if contact was made in person). Dr. Ada Zohar of the Ruppin Academic Center was the lone individual who was willing to pass out my flyer to her students, but this did not garner any participants, which she warned me would likely be the case because most of the students at the Ruppin Academic Center are not English-speakers.

After still having zero Israeli participants on day 14 of my allotted 28 days of research, I handed my recruitment flyer to the manager of the hostel I was staying at and told her the trouble I was having getting any response from potential Israeli participants. She took a recruitment flyer from me and immediately contacted her own network of people. The IRB was informed of the procedural adjustments and no formal revision to the approval was requested. Within 48 hours of the hostel manager reaching out to her network, I had 15 Israelis contact me for interviews, ten of whom followed up and actually completed an interview with me. Every Israeli interview took place in Jerusalem at a cafe, restaurant, or secluded location of the participant's choosing.

While all of the Israeli interviews took place in one city, the Palestinian interviews were much more spread out. Three of the interviews took place in Bethlehem, three of the interviews took place in Ramallah, and one of the interviews took place over a Skype meeting. One of the Bethlehem interviews took place at a Banksy gift shop along the Israeli-Palestinian wall, one of the other Bethlehem interviews took place in a home in a refugee camp, another Bethlehem interview took place at a restaurant, and all three interviews in Ramallah took place outside the student cafe at Birzeit University. The Skype interview took place while I was in Nazareth and the participant was in Jericho.

During the interviews, no recording devices were used, as per the IRB approval for methodology. Instead, I wrote notes based on the participants' responses. I rarely transcribed exact quotes from the participants and my notes instead reflected the central stories and the overarching themes that the participants were emphasizing. Despite all being English-speaking, there was a communication gap as colloquialisms differed and their English had been learned secondary to Hebrew (if Jewish or Israeli) or Arabic (if Palestinian).

By the seventh Israeli interview and the sixth Palestinian interview, it appeared to me that I had already achieved some theme saturation: albeit a small sample size of each population, the interviews each appeared to have similar – if not identical – responses to my questions. However, because I was not analyzing the data as I collected it, I continued collecting as much data as I could. I stopped collecting data because my time to do so had run its course, not because I believed I had achieved theme saturation.

Data Analysis

Saldaña (2016) explains "a code in qualitative inquiry is most often a word or short phrase that symbolically assigns a summative, salient, essence-capturing, and/or evocative attribute" in accordance with the data, which can consist of "participant observation field notes" (p. 4). The idea is to describe the "critical link between data collection and their explanation of meaning" (p. 4). Saldaña emphasizes that there is no one single correct way to achieve this, and that the individuals driving the study determine the appropriate coding. In this way, I strived to ensure that the way I coded most accurately reflected the voice of the participants, while also maintaining the confidentiality I had promised them.

Coding Procedure

After collecting all data, I created a description of the participants and a summary of each of the interviews. These summaries can be found in Appendix B. To supplement the direction of the coding, I input these summaries into NVivo and generated a WordCloud to highlight the most frequently used words as a cross-reference to my interpretation of the themes that had appeared (Diagram 3). Only 18 words appeared more than 15 times (i.e., approximately once per interview) and can be found in Table 5. Unsurprisingly, the most common hits were "trauma" (40 references), "Israeli" (39), "conflict" (36), and "Palestinian" (31).

DIAGRAM 3: WordCloud (NVivo)

TABLE 5: Top Word Frequency (NVivo)

Word	Length	Count	Weighted Percentage ∨
trauma	6	40	1.35%
israeli	7	39	1.31%
conflict	8	36	1.21%
palestinian	11	31	1.04%
believes	8	27	0.91%
arabs	5	26	0.88%
jews	4	21	0.71%
jewish	6	20	0.67%
old	3	20	0.67%
feels	5	19	0.64%
palestinians	12	19	0.64%
people	6	19	0.64%
year	4	18	0.61%
gaza	4	17	0.57%
israel	6	17	0.57%
religious	9	17	0.57%
like	4	16	0.54%
parents	7	16	0.54%
friends	7	15	0.51%

Other frequent word usages included feeling-related words, like "believes," "report," and "religious." Words like "killed," "suffering," "traumatic," "bomb," "IDF," "Holocaust," and "war" highlight the tense environment that most of these participants lived in. Words that denote family members were often used, but perhaps the most surprising frequent family-based role was "grandpa." The research was focused on immediate family only (i.e., parents/guardians), yet many of the discussions led to conversation about the participants' grandfathers. One curiously frequent word was "I10," which is in reference to Israeli Participant #10. It is hard to determine if this is simply because I used "I10" instead of pronouns "he/him/his" in his summary, or if it is because I reported more details about his life, perhaps revealing a preferential bias I had towards his story.

After considering these observations, I reflected upon the summaries again and tried to step back and understand the collective story that was being told by Israelis, Palestinians, *and* Israelis and Palestinians combined. I found statements that were made by participants and then connected those statements to other participants' statements. I considered these statements in light of the two research questions, 1) "how does Transgenerational Trauma Transmission

(TTT) manifest in Israeli and Palestinian young adults?" and 2) "how does religious identity affect the lenses of Israelis and Palestinians in conflict?"

Recurring topics were then broken down into the following 12 categories: "TTT does not necessarily create hate," "those with TTT have lessened faith," "those with TTT have relational barriers," "instances of direct trauma," "instances of indirect trauma," "trauma experienced by grandparents/parents," "somatic manifestations of trauma," "resentment of Palestinian Authority," "anxiety around IDF," "anxiety around non-military Israelis or non-military Palestinians," "contempt for conflict," and "commentary on conflict." Relevant categories were then packaged together into seven specific themes.

Thematic Analysis

Analysis of the patterns within Israelis' and Palestinians' responses revealed seven recurring themes that were largely true for most participants, regardless of their ethnic or religious identification: (a) those dealing with TTT do not recognize their trauma as clinically significant; (b) those dealing with TTT display behavioral changes and negative somatic manifestations rather than psychological symptoms; (c) those dealing with TTT have loss of faith; (d) those dealing with TTT have relational barriers with those belonging to the group that their elders have had conflict with; (e) those dealing with TTT do not necessarily hate those belonging to the group that their elders have had conflict with; (f) Israelis and Palestinians have contempt for the conflict and resentment towards the government(s) that exacerbate the conflict; and (g) Israelis and Palestinians do not believe there is a solution to the conflict that does not involve war.

Theme One: Trauma Not Viewed as Clinically Significant by Participants

Despite Katz and Lavee's (2004) assertion that nearly 100% of those in Israel experience trauma, only three of the 17 participants reported experiencing trauma. Of the ten Israeli participants, seven of them described experiencing symptoms or experiences that westerners would consider "traumatic" (like rocket blasts or getting caught in crossfire), but only two of the Israeli participants actually identified these experiences as traumatic or understood them to be potentially trauma-inducing situations. Of the 17 participants, only two individuals (Israeli Eight and Israeli Nine) recognized their exposure to the conflict as something that was clinically significant enough to qualify for PTSD. Despite having been exposed to gunshots, rockets, bus bombings, and loss of family and friends to acts of war, the other 15 participants did not believe their trauma to be clinically significant. When the reason for this was stated, it was often because the participant felt that their exposure to trauma was minimal in comparison to their elders, most usually a parent or grandparent. For instance, Palestinian Three had been exposed to gunshots, gas bombs, combat helicopters, and rockets throughout her life. Growing up, she used to quickly lie down on the ground to avoid bullets being shot into her window from a nearby Israeli settlement. Palestinian Three said she still gets nervous around Israeli checkpoints and is "more afraid of the world." Despite this, Palestinian Three was adamant that she does not have PTSD because she believes her experiences to be minimal compared to that of her elders: her grandpa was shot near the heart and now "one wrong move could end him," and her father spent a decade in an IDF prison. Likewise, Palestinian One witnessed the IDF destroy several homes as a child, which prompted him to lose sleep in fear that he would lose his own, yet he does not recognize himself as being in a post-traumatic state.

These sentiments were not confined to Palestinians: Israelis also expressed these beliefs. Israeli Ten comes from a family with a long history of military service to Israel. In the IDF, he was tasked with finding terror tunnels and hunting down Palestinian suspects who were building these tunnels, and he has been in combat. When asked if he had ever experienced anything that might be considered potentially traumatic, Israeli Ten shrugged off the question and responded, "Just rockets and gunshots." He did not feel that his experiences were as significant as his grandpa's, who served in five Israeli conflicts, including the precipitous 1948 War.

Likewise, Israeli Four explained the conflict was always "felt" while growing up and remembered many conversations starting with the question, "did you hear what happened?" She recalled breaking down into tears when she saw her grandpa's car that had been riddled

116

with bullets; her grandpa was shot in the leg during that incident. Some of her teachers and schoolmates also were killed from other attacks during the intifada. Despite all this, the only "trauma" she reported was from five months earlier when she had been in a moderate motorcycle accident in Vietnam.

When asked about any trauma she faced while growing up, Israeli One stated throughout the interview that she was not exposed to any. However, three minutes before the 60-minute allotted time expired, she suddenly remembered being in a settlement just outside of Ramallah on New Year's Day during the Second Intifada and having several gunshots sprayed in her direction, including one that hit the building she was staying in. Similarly, she grew up in a time period when her friends' family members were killed and Arab terrorists frequently blew up busses, and as a result, still gets nervous when a lone Arab gets onto a bus she is commuting on. Despite this, she does not consider this to truly be "trauma," and instead considers the events that her grandma went through during the Holocaust (i.e., frequently hiding under the bed when sirens alarmed) to be trauma. Similarly, Israeli Five remembered daydreaming as a child about what it would be like to be killed in the conflict, but does not consider herself to have clinical trauma and instead refers to such psychological processes as "indirect trauma."

Israeli Seven was an IDF paratrooper who was a part of the 2014 military operation Protective Edge which left thousands of Gazans dead. As a result of his combat experience, Israeli Seven claimed he still gets fearful when he hears Arabic being spoken. However, his father was a soldier during the Second Lebanon War whom internalized any trauma he may have endured. In hindsight, Israeli Seven recognizes that some of his father's behavior was the result of post-traumatic behavior, and he only came to this conclusion after recognizing similarities to his own post-war behaviors – yet Israeli Seven does not believe himself to have clinical trauma.

As a child during the intifada, Israeli Six endured "massive" attacks near his home and claimed that he still is struck with fear when he hears Arabic because that is the language he heard just before attacks while in the IDF. Despite this, he does not see this peculiar mindset to be of clinical significance and instead referred to it as a "survival instinct."

Finally, Israeli Two has faced several potentially traumatic situations, from being arrested in Iraq for backpacking in a restricted area to having a close Palestinian friend blow himself up in a terror attack in 2016. Instead of being upset by the latter event, Israeli Two leaked information about the attack to the media based on information he knew from being friends with the individual. He claimed to be otherwise unaffected by the suicide attack, referring to it as more of an "adventure." When asked specifically what he considers to be a traumatic experience in his life, he only referred to being traumatized by the "stonewall truths that have become decayed" in his life, most notably his Jewish faith, which has led him to distrust institutions and feel betrayed by his parents.

Theme Two: Participants Had Physical and Behavioral Manifestations of Trauma Rather Than Psychological

Nearly all trauma assessments focus on psychological dysfunction, but several participants expressed that those who have endured extreme trauma often have behavioral and somatic ailments, such as cancer, ulcers, diabetes, and poor heart health. Palestinian Seven reported that his mother randomly lost her eyesight one day and he still did not know how it happened. Palestinian Six reported that her face would "turn red for days" whenever she found herself near shootouts while growing up. Previously mentioned was Israeli Four, who claimed that the only real trauma she has faced was a motorcycle accident – something that physically and empirically affected her body, unlike other trauma she minimized.

There was anecdotal evidence worth considering as well. In a passing conversation, I was told about a man who nearly was blown up by a rocket and rather than developing post-trauma symptoms, he was soon after diagnosed with diabetes. While in the field, I met another researcher from New Zealand who told me about a close colleague who contracted cancer in his native Iraq after a particularly traumatic encounter. Another Palestinian that I met (who was too old to participate in my study) lost her dad to a heart attack the night he was told that his son was being tortured in an Israeli prison.

Israeli Ten spoke to this phenomenon and noted that trauma is found "not in the stories," but in the behaviors of people. He cited the example of his father who has a fear of heights, and noted that he did not inherit his father's fear of heights, but rather, his anxiety. During the debriefing period in which Israeli Ten was exposed to the true purpose of the study, he encouraged the research to stop being so focused on the internalization of TTT (i.e., how TTT affects thoughts/beliefs) and instead look for the trauma to be manifested in a trauma-sufferer's actions. Palestinian Five was the most vivid example of this pronouncement, stating that he once had a medical emergency in which he needed to go to the hospital, but refused to go because he did not want to deal with having to go through the cumbersome IDF checkpoint or interact with demeaning IDF soldiers.

Theme Three: Participants Have Significant Loss of Faith

Perhaps the most clearly recurring theme was a loss of faith in the religion that the participant was raised to believe, as well as religion in general: 16 of the 17 participants (94.1%) were raised in religious households, but only six of the 17 participants (35.3%) claimed to be religious, and only four of the participants (23.5%) still practiced their faith (i.e., observed prayer and still read holy texts). Three of the six Israeli participants who were raised religious but rejected the major tenets of their Jewish faith (50.0%) and all six of the Palestinian participants who were raised religious but rejected the major tenets of their faith (100%) had what could be described as a "loss of faith" in which they did not become hostile to religion but also did not find value in practicing it. Three of the six Israeli participants who were raised religious but rejected the major tenets of their Jewish faith (50.0%) had what could be described as a stark "rejection of faith" in which they consciously came to a decision to apostatize from their religion. This was an intriguing theme because Katz and Lavee (2004) accounted for nearly 100% of Israel's population to identify as religious, but my research indicated less than 25% actually were religious. This discrepancy could not be explained by lack of a religious education, as 15 of the 17 participants (88.24%) were familiar with the relatively-obscure prophecy of Gog and Magog.

Palestinian One, Palestinian Two, Palestinian Four, Palestinian Five, and Palestinian Seven were all raised in Islam, but consider themselves nonreligious. Palestinian Five added that he prefers Fatah to Hamas, as Fatah is a secular government and Hamas is a religious-based one. Only one of the Palestinian participants made a point to emphasize that she is still dedicated to Islam. The only Palestinian who was raised in a Christian household and self-identified as a Christian explained that she "believes in all religions" as being true.

Israeli One, Israeli Two, Israeli Three, Israeli Four, Israeli Six, and Israeli Ten were all raised in Judaism and are now either atheist, agnostic, or otherwise nonreligious. Israeli Two and Israeli Four came from deeply-rooted Jewish families; Israeli Two reported that his grandpa and father have been some of the most influential rabbis in Atlanta, Georgia, and that he comes from a powerful rabbinic dynasty. However, Israeli Two is now agnostic and the only truth he knows for sure is that "I believe I exist," and even this conclusion took much critical thought and consideration to arrive to. Israeli Four stated that "as a child, I put my faith in God. But as an adult, now I put my faith in the IDF." She reported that she had "come out" to her mother as an atheist in a recent "National Coming Out Day," which is typically reserved for individuals telling their family that they are gay/lesbian. However, the symbolism proved to have powerful meaning to Israeli Four, which is why she chose this day to announce her atheism to her Jewish family.

Israeli Seven was an outlier to this theme. He was raised in an environment hostile to Judaism: his parents would purposely and publicly defy the Torah by doing the opposite of what it commands. For example, they would eat pork every Yom Kippur. Despite this, Israeli Seven is now nonreligious rather than anti-religious.

Theme Four: Participants Have Relational Barriers with Descendants of Elders' Enemies

As Palestinian Seven noted, whenever someone suffers the loss of a loved one, the incident creates a grudge between the mourner and the individual or group that the mourner perceives to be responsible for the loss. Many of the participants displayed that their relationships with their so-called enemies had stark barriers. While most Palestinians reported feelings of nervousness around IDF soldiers, Palestinian participants did not report feelings of anxiety around everyday Israelis. Conversely, many of the Israeli participants reported feeling nervous around Arabs, regardless of what they were wearing or how they looked. This is likely due to the fact that most Israeli-on-Palestinian violence is committed by IDF soldiers, whereas most (if not all) of Palestinian-on-Israeli violence is committed by individual Palestinian entities (as opposed to the Palestinian military). Additionally, Palestinians frequently committed suicide bombings in contrast to Israelis who largely have not engaged in this type of warfare.

As a result of these dynamics, Palestinian Two and Palestinian Seven both reported not having any Jewish friends, and Israeli Six, Israeli Eight, and Israeli Nine stated they are not friends with Arabs and/or Muslims. Palestinian Six was raised to fear Jews because "we have stones; they have guns." While growing up, the IDF stole merchandise from her dad's business and she would hide when the IDF would show up, adding "some Jews are without humanity." Palestinian Five noted that he is friends with Jews, but that he obviously would not be friends with any Zionist Jews. Israeli Ten emphasized that while Jews do generally have empathy for Palestinians, Jews generally do not trust them. Israeli Nine added that she recognizes that Palestinians are suffering and that that is "sad," but asserts that they "have not been partners in peace." Similarly, Israeli Eight finds it hard to connect with Palestinians because he cannot be friends with people who deny the Jewish narrative, and he has found that many Palestinians refuse to even acknowledge the existence of the Holocaust. When I pressed him on whether or not this might actually be true or was perhaps just a fallacy he believed, he responded "I don't need to tell you what I believe. Go look up the official stance of [Palestinian Authority] President [Mahmoud] Abbas regarding the Shoah. The Palestinians elected this man as their leader." After the interview, I did as he asked and found that President Abbas does, in fact, deny that the Holocaust ever happened and even wrote his PhD dissertation in support of this stance.

The relational divide between Jews and Palestinians appeared to be taught by schools and parents alike. Israeli Eight asserted that the Jewish mantra is to "enjoy life" while Palestinians' mantra is to "kill people," citing the idea that Jews mourn their lost loved ones as victims while Palestinians celebrate their lost loved ones as martyrs. Israeli Five was taught that Arabs are "inherently bad," and that this belief was somewhat solidified by several instances of Arab men sexually harassing her as a young woman. Israeli One also expressed that she believes Arab men to be "sexist," citing that she has had several issues of Arab men sexually harassing her as well. Israeli Four was raised to believe that Arabs are liars and thieves, and though she now recognizes these sentiments as racist, the ideas are still ingrained.

Several Jews noted that even though they were raised to use caution around Arabs, their real-life experiences are what most influenced their anxiety around Arabs. Israeli Five explained that she was raised in her religiously Jewish school to be wary of Arabs, but that "after getting shot at by Palestinians, the lesson is no longer even needed." Israeli One is uncomfortable if an Arab gets on a bus she is riding. Israeli Nine is likewise suspicious of Arabs who have backpacks or coats. She also avoids the Damascus Gate of the Old City because it is the main entrance to the Muslim Quarter, and she asserted that most Jews avoid this entrance. Israeli Seven expressed that he becomes nervous when he hears Arabic phrases as it reminds him of his time in Gaza with the IDF; when I asked if he ever had any good experiences with Gaza Palestinians, he stated "I've never been around a Gaza Palestinian I wasn't shooting at."

Several of the participants displayed that relational barriers had been built within their own in-group. Israeli One believes that the Jewish narrative is inherently racist because it asserts that Jews are superior to all other races. She has a Zionist brother who has been arrested for terrorism and she has disowned him as a result. She lamented how quickly he was radicalized, stating "at [age] 13, he was listening to Backstreet Boys and at 16, he was a religious zealot." Israeli Two stated that he distrusts his Jewish family and all institutions, whether Jewish, Israeli, Palestinian, or Muslim. Palestinian Six was angry at her sister for getting pregnant while living in the West Bank, stating that she told her that it was "shallow" of her to want to bring children into the sociopolitical situation in Palestine. Israeli Eight has a clinical diagnosis of severe PTSD and has exhibited suicidal behavior, but he feels he cannot tell his family about his struggles because "once you tell them the truth, they pity you for life." He has dialed his mom in moments of extreme hopelessness, only to hang up before she answers because he does not want to change the dynamic of their relationship by telling her what he has faced.

Theme Five: Participants Do Not Necessarily Hate the Descendants of Elders' Enemies

While relational barriers did exist across participants' groups, not a single participant used the word "hate" when describing their feelings towards their enemies, but occasionally did use the word "hate" when describing what they assumed to be their enemies' feelings towards them. However, there was an overwhelming sense that participants generally wished they could have peace with their enemies. Israeli Six, who was previously identified as having developed an innate "survival instinct" of fear when he hears Arabic because of combat experiences with Palestinians – emphasized that he wants Palestine to have statehood. Israeli Four likewise asserted that Palestinians should be given some of their land back by Israel, and noted that she would support this option even if it meant that her parents and sister would lose the land they have claimed in the West Bank.

Palestinian One, when asked how he views Jews, stated that he sees them as brothers and sisters, adding that "we are all one" race. Likewise, Palestinian Two was raised to believe that Jews are "no different" than Muslims. Palestinian Five's father and grandma had several confrontations with the IDF, but he does not have excessive animosity towards IDF, stating that their actions and the entire conflict is actually rooted in the IDF being scared for their own safety which, in turn, prompts them to preemptively shoot. Palestinian Seven stated that he was told to be cautious around Jews because of the political climate, but that Jews are not inherently bad.

Israelis had similar sentiments in regards to Palestinians: Israeli Four referred to Palestinians and Arabs as her "cousins." Israeli Two stated he actually has more Palestinian friends than Israeli friends as he lives in Bethlehem. This is an illegal act, but he says he does it because he wants to understand their perspective and assimilate with them. Israeli Seven (who was formerly an IDF paratrooper tasked with hunting down Palestinian terror suspects in Gaza) said that he actually feels sorry for Palestinians, and noted this to be especially true for Palestinians living in Gaza as he empathizes and feels sorrow for the way they are suffering. He estimated that 90% of West Bank Arabs want peace. Israeli Ten was in direct combat against Palestinian Gazans during his IDF service but is now friends with many Gazans, and believes that someday, war will break out and he will be called back into service and have to kill his Gazan friends. He noted, though, that he has no animosity towards them and that "it's not personal, we're just standing on principles."

Theme Six: Contempt for Conflict and the Governments That Exacerbate It

Rather than directing their hate towards each other, Israelis and Palestinians focus their enmity towards those actually responsible for the continuation of the conflict: politicians. Most participants felt the conflict to be "unnecessary" and "annoying" at best, or a misguided "crime against humanity" at worst. Even the participants who identified the need for the conflict felt that the way it has played out has been mismanaged by both Israeli and Palestinian political parties.

Israeli Four referred to the Israeli and Palestinian leadership as "stupid" for their inability to move towards peace, and added that PA leadership specifically is deceptive and cannot be trusted, which makes it difficult on the Israeli government. Israeli One – who is agnostic and opposed to religion – stated she was annoyed with Arab governments that attempt to take holy land away from the Jews who first attached religious significance to the land. Israeli Eight was frustrated towards the Israeli government for agreeing to the Oslo Accords, which he called "the biggest mistake in the history of Israel," and equated it to inviting a convicted rapist into one's own home. However, he described the PA as the bigger contributor to the conflict and alleged that Palestinian leaders purposely try to keep their people ignorant of the real issues.

Israeli Nine also labeled the PA as the "selfish" party who will never allow the conflict to end because, while Israeli's endgame is peace, the PA's endgame is proving that they are justified to hate Israel. She gave the example of Israel providing Gaza financial and resource assistance in 2005 that was intended to benefit the Gazan people through education and other necessities, but instead, the money was utilized to fund terror tunnels that the IDF had to demolish.

While Israelis are predisposed to favoring their own government over the PA, the disapproval towards the PA was actually shared by all of the Palestinian participants, too. As one Palestinian participant described, there are actually three factions (not just two) within the Israeli-Palestinian Conflict: Israelis, Palestinians, and the Palestinian Authority. Another participant described the Palestinian Authority as a "poison" to both Israelis and Palestinians. A particularly striking statistic was that nine of the ten Israeli participants had either positive or mixed feelings about the Israeli government's concern for its people, whereas seven of the seven Palestinian participants had feelings of abandonment by the Palestinian Authority.

Palestinian Three felt strongly that the PA underestimates and undermines Palestinians' ability and right to protest, and emphasized that her anger is towards Fatah, Hamas, and the PA rather than Israelis. Palestinian Four called the conflict "fishy" in that it seems to benefit both the Israeli government and PA, and he provided the example of Palestinians being imprisoned by the PA after they had already served jailtime in IDF custody for the same crime. Palestinian Five likewise vocalized that he sometimes wonders if the IDF and the PA are secretly operating together for some hidden purpose. Palestinian One and Palestinian Six were the only Palestinian participants to vocalize that they still felt like peace could be achieved by the PA, but both of them also noted that they do not have enough faith in this belief to stick around and are actively seeking opportunities to leave the country.

Israeli Two – who is the Israeli participant who is illegally living in Bethlehem – was the only Israeli who did not feel the Israeli government was working in the best interests of its people. He said the current conflict is "an echo of the original issues," and characterized the conflict as a "brand" that is not unlike a sports rivalry in which both "teams" benefit from their dislike for each other. He used the Yankees/Red Sox rivalry as an analogy to the Israeli-Palestinian Conflict, as people now blindly cheer for their "team" and against their rival despite not having been present for the impetus for the rivalry in the first place. Israeli Two stated that it provides an identity for both Jews and Muslims, and that unlike other Arabs and Muslims in the Middle East, Palestinians are devoid of an identity without the Israeli-Palestinian Conflict. Israeli Two asserted that Israeli Prime Minister Netanyahu also benefits from keeping the conflict aflame, and that both Israel and Palestine greatly benefit financially from keeping the conflict conflagrant. He cited the separation wall between Palestine and Israel as a prime example: tourists from all over the world come to take "selfies" in front of the boundary, treating the war zone like it is "Disneyland." Israeli Two explained the conflict to be a "stimulus and response" apparatus in which Netanyahu "taps into Jewish fears" in order to promote his stance on the conflict, and that Israelis and Palestinians derive a level of satisfaction from "being right" because of their allegiance to their ethnic identities, governments, and religious roots. Still, Israeli Two reported that he feels emotionally-connected to his culture and traditions and is not hostile towards religion. Despite rejecting his Jewish upbringing, living in Bethlehem, and assimilating to Palestinian culture, he is grieved when Muslim culture takes Jewish history – which came thousands of years before theirs – and alters it to fit their narratives. As an example, he cited the Temple Mount, stating, "Muslims believe the Temple Mount is holy. Why do they believe it is holy? Well, because it was holy to Jews first." He believes that Arab Muslims tend to view the world in a black-and-white dichotomous lens that is more rooted in "dramatic effect rather than empirical evidence," and that this plays out in the way the PA exacerbates the conflict.

Theme Seven: Belief That the Conflict Cannot Be Solved Without Another War

None of the participants had a positive outlook for the future of Israeli-Palestinian relations. Israeli One called the conflict "unsolvable" and said she does not think much about it anymore because it is "not worth [her] time." Israeli Six referenced the Battle of Gog and Magog as being the eventual outcome of the conflict, and said that in order to avoid the conflict being elevated to this level, it is important to keep lame-duck politicians in office if they have proven an ability to control their people, even if those politicians happen to be tyrants. He referenced the arrest and execution of Saddam Hussein as a huge mistake by the United States because they killed the only leader who had a proven track record of being able to control Iraqi Arabs. Palestinian Seven likewise said the conflict will never be solved, but simply "managed forever." Israeli Two also stated that the United States actually exacerbates the conflict by "projecting their own problems onto the conflict" and imagining themselves as participants of the conflict (which they decidedly are not). Israeli Nine was also resigned to the idea that the conflict really does not have a solution and that she copes with this reality by volunteering for peace missions, which helps her combat feelings of hopelessness and helplessness. Israeli Eight similarly explained that the conflict has no alternative than to simply remain in a stalemate because, "Hebrews don't speak Arabic and Arabs don't speak Hebrew; how are we supposed to talk?"

Some participants conceded that the conflict could be solved in theory, but that it will not because it requires concessions that are too steep for either side. Israeli Five explained that economic cooperation is the solution to the conflict, but it will not happen because Israel neither trusts Palestine nor has a willingness to lose anything. Palestinian Five said that the only solution would be if the Israeli government and PA would be dissolved and rebuilt as one party, but that such a cooperation is basically a statistical impossibility. Israeli Three said that a peace treaty would require Israel to give land back to Palestinians, which most likely would mean giving the Golan Heights back to Palestine and putting Israeli military in a topographically untenable position. Israel seized the Golan Heights as part of the 1967 Six-Day War, and Israeli Three noted that returning that land to Palestine would result in a similar bloodshed because of the strategic advantage it provides. Israeli Seven echoed these exact sentiments, stating that history has already seen how Palestine would use the Golan Heights against Israel. He believes the conflict will erupt into war, and that he will be called back into service with the IDF to fight Syria, Lebanon, and/or Gaza. Israeli Ten also believed that such a war is inevitable, and was the only Israeli to state he believed that Palestine would win this particular outbreak and that it would result in Israel and

Palestine merging into one country under the PA. While he conceded that he may be wrong about the result of the war, he was adamant that the Jewish connection to the land of Israel needs to be recognized before any kind of peace can be achieved.

Operationalization of Transgenerational Trauma Transmission

This study assented to the post-trauma symptoms that were identified in previous research on TTT, and in Chapter 2, an operational definition based off of the current literature was created. However, based on participants' responses in this study, it appears that additional qualifiers have been missed. Specifically, it would be beneficial for the definition to also include TTT's potential influence on behaviors, physical health, faith, and meaning-making processes. As such, a revised operational definition of TTT is proposed. Transgenerational Trauma Transmission can be described as when:

A. A member of the person's immediate family (i.e., parent, grandparent, sibling) has been exposed to a traumatic event that involved potential death or potential injury, and later recounted the event with inclusion of these details:
   a. The offender's perceived race or religion
   b. The setting (e.g., bus stop, shopping mall, house of worship, etc.)
   c. The perceived meaning of the encounter
B. After the recounting of the traumatic event(s), the person experienced some of the following:
   a. Cautiousness or avoidance of the perceived race or religion of the offender
   b. Avoidance of the setting
   c. Persistent thoughts about the event that did not happen to them
   d. Significant behavioral changes
   e. Somatic illnesses
   f. Loss of faith in religion
   g. Belief (unconscious or conscious) that they will never experience anything as significantly traumatic as their loved one did

Summary

Along with the addition to the working operational definition of TTT, this chapter identified seven themes through the course of my 17 interviews: (a) those dealing with TTT do not recognize their trauma as clinically significant; (b) those dealing with TTT display behavioral changes and negative somatic manifestations rather than psychological symptoms; (c) those dealing with TTT have loss of faith; (d) those dealing with TTT have relational barriers with those belonging to the group that their elders have had conflict with; (e) those dealing with TTT do not necessarily hate those belonging to the group that their elders have had conflict with; (f) Israelis and Palestinians have contempt for the conflict and resentment towards the government(s) that exacerbate the conflict; and (g) Israelis and Palestinians do not believe there is a viable solution to the conflict that does not involve war. Succinctly, participants perceived the conflict to largely be a political and ethnic one (rather than religious) that is intensified by the ineptitude and/or scheming of Israel and Palestinian political leaders. Chapter 5 explores the interpretations and implications from these findings.

Chapter 5: Discussion

Chapter Overview

This research study set out to better understand the way trauma is transmitted across multiple generations of Israelis and Palestinians, to include how religion influenced the lenses of such individuals. This final chapter will now explain the conclusions that were gleaned from this data and, just as importantly, what could not be concluded from the data. It will also attempt to identify the shortcomings of this study that ultimately prevented it from achieving its full potential, and how future studies can implement solutions to overcome these issues.

Interpretation of Findings

Phenomenological studies are concerned with constructs that are missing, as what is absent can be just as important as what is present (Smith et al., 2009). In this sense, participants who lacked religious conviction may be revealing something about TTT as much as those who are adherent to their faith. The reality was that my study showed more evidence that religious identity plays nearly *no role* in the meaning-making processes for those in Israel and Palestine. Granted, most of my participants had displayed a loss of faith, but even for those who tightly clung to their religious roots, their religious background did not appear to affect their vantage. Religion simply seems to be appreciated differently in the Middle East than in the western world.

My second research question, "How does religious identity affect the lenses of Israelis and Palestinians in conflict?," was rooted in the assumption that religious identity already affected participants' outlook on life in general. In the western world, religion is holistic; in Israel and Palestine, there is seemingly a separation between religion and the events one endures. Practically speaking, a religious westerner may say, "God is my healer and will see me through to victory," while a religious individual in Israel or Palestine may not place such an expectation on God to deal with their personal situation. My own upbringing and biases reflected what can be described as a religious fatalism: "God is sovereign and *therefore He will protect me.*" None of the participants expressed such a view, and the attitude was more

130

along the lines of, "God is sovereign and *therefore He allows bad things happen to me.*"

Prior to traveling for data collection, I was presented with a "battle of two narratives" between Israelis and Palestinians. In one sense, there was one overarching Jewish narrative (i.e., "The Chosen People") that was in competition with an overarching Palestinian narrative (i.e., "The Right to Return to Jerusalem"). As such, many of the historical events in the conflict have already been affixed a specific meaning. For example, the Israeli narrative of the Six-Day War is one of military triumph, but one Israeli was hesitant to accept that narrative, considering it more-or-less to be propaganda. However, this same participant did not dare to publicly challenge the Israeli narrative of the war as it was a historical event that had an established meaning. Likewise, the Palestinian narrative for the intifadas is one of ethnic pride – that is, Palestinians rose up and tried to take back what they believed to be theirs. A few Palestinian participants rejected this narrative, and yet were reticent to publicly express their frustration for their government's role in perpetuating violence because the participants' voices would be inconsistent with what has become the Palestinian narrative. So in this sense, the meaning of significant historical events in the Israeli-Palestinian Conflict has already been established and cannot be challenged.

These narratives are at the deepest root of the conflict, to the point that some participants referred to their counterparts' narratives as "lies." Undeniably, there are facts in the Israeli narrative that are plainly incompatible with the facts that Palestinians operate off of (and vice versa), and until Israeli students and Palestinian students sit in the same classrooms together and learn from the same textbooks, this tension will continue to exist between the two narratives.

However, in a much deeper sense, there are countless narratives. After all, the conflict is not between just one or two parties: the conflict is made up of the 10,000,000+ individuals living in Israel and Palestine. What I found was a battle of countless narratives – it is an oversimplification to lump these together as either "Israeli" or "Palestinian" overarching narratives, as if the Israeli-Palestinian Conflict was reduced to an American football matchup (Keret, 2016).

If we insist on using this analogy, we must start seeing the conflict as a full league with 30+ different teams all vying for the championship across a long season rather than two teams competing in a sole three-hour matchup. Instead of the conventional (and oversimplified) "Israelis hate Palestinians / Palestinians hate Israelis" narrative, I found a much more complicated narrative in which both Israelis and Palestinians have formed caution, resentment, and distrust towards each other – not necessarily hate.

As is usually the case, there remains a divide between theory and practice: Katz and Lavee (2004) insisted that most Israelis are Jewish, but now I am not sure what that even means. In most literature, there is no distinction made between a Jew by ethnicity, a practicing Jew, or a Jew wrestling with his/her faith. Israeli One criticized that my study was too ambitious and that there are too many individual sects of Judaism and Islam to simply say I am studying "Israelis and Palestinians" without breaking down the nuances of each specific sub-culture. She noted that if I were to have asked a Gaza Arab the same questions as an East Jerusalem Arab, it would likely have completely changed the direction of the research as the Jerusalemite Arab has likely had several peaceful encounters with Israelis, while Gazans only see Israelis through their scopes. She said the same is also true of Jews: a Jew near Gaza would likely have a wildly different outlook than those living in a major city. Israeli One noted the adage, "If you ask two Israelis about something, you'll get three opinions."

Implication

I leave future researchers with one grand implication: it is time to rethink our definition of trauma; the clinical definition of PTSD is inadequate for those in non-western contexts. As such, symptomology ought to be appreciated from a construct universalism perspective. Both the western world and the Middle East inherently understand what is meant by the concept of "trauma," but just like the word is pronounced differently in English than it is in Hebrew or Arabic, so it is different in its manifestation, too.

Participants did not express potential symptoms of trauma in the traditional way. Yet, because they could only view trauma through

132

the westernized lens they were presented with (i.e., PTSD), they did not believe their manifestations of trauma to be clinically significant. My data indicated that the perception of trauma was almost entirely external, and post-traumatic symptoms were conceptualized as being "survival instinct" rather than trauma. The idea of "trauma" seemed confined to when a loved one faced a life-threatening situation, but when the same type of event happened to the participant, it was considered a part of daily life. In fact, the participants expressed more emotional connection to the life-threatening events that happened to loved ones than they did towards events that occurred to themselves. Some of this can be explained by the fact that Israel is a blend of collectivism and individualism on Hofstede's cultural dimensions (Vaughn, 2010), but it does not account for the way individual victims of trauma could be affected physiologically.

PTSD may very well have its place in the Middle East, but there is something else going on that is largely unaccounted for. I called this phenomenon Transgenerational Trauma Transmission (TTT), but the label itself is not important. What is important is that this phenomenon becomes understood so well that a clinician can differentiate between symptoms of PTSD and symptoms of TTT. To be sure, there will be overlap, and symptoms of both phenomena can exist at the same time together. But the field of psychology must stop using PTSD as the only modality of trauma; the field of psychology must do no (more) harm.

Limitations

I consciously attempted to shed my western assumptions as I designed my research, but even with this at the forefront of my mind, I could not escape the way western conceptualizations formed my theory. I went to Israel and Palestine with the intent to research trauma without my western flag showing, but then I asked questions like "do you have nightmares" and "do you have anxiety" during the interviews. In hindsight, for a study that was intended to be culturally neutral, such questions are laughable. Instead, I should have not espoused an assumption that post-trauma symptoms would necessarily manifest in the same manner as is seen with PTSD in the western world. Questions about physical illness and deep-seeded attitudes may have been more appropriate. To this end, the most frequent recurring word in my interview notes was "trauma," and it is now impossible to ascertain if this word came up so frequently because I introduced it or because the participant would have described their experiences using that specific word.

Clearly, there was an inherent limitation in that trauma (as defined in the western world) did not seem to translate well enough to the concept of trauma in the Middle East. As a result, the literature review that drove the premise of this study did not even represent Israeli or Palestinian voices well enough. This was not by design. The libraries accessible to me for this study scarcely had scholarly Israeli literature and there currently exists a dearth of peer-reviewed Palestinian literature. The Israeli Psychological Association is young (Welfel & Khamush, 2012), and there exists no Palestinian equivalent psychological association. As a consequence, the literature that drove this study was largely rooted in western thought.

However, the western concepts that *were* available to me were not even investigated in full. When talking about Israel's penchant for dealing with several conflicts at once, one Israeli participant noted, "Jews heal faster." Tedeschi and Calhoun (2009) offered the idea of post-traumatic growth, in which an individual's resiliency helps them to make meaning of (and eventually overcome) traumas that they have previously faced. In many cases, those who have post-traumatic growth find their traumatic situations to be a source of strength. Research has already shown that Israelis have displayed resiliency; Denham (2008) observed that descendants of survivors of the Holocaust were able to overcome post-traumatic symptoms if their parents had been able to make meaning out of the tragedy. Unfortunately, this topic was not explored fully enough to draw any conclusions regarding it, which is a missed opportunity as there is almost no published research on Palestinian resiliency.

Still, the most glaring limitation of this study is the small sample size. Interviewing more participants would have revealed different themes (or expounded on the themes already presented). The reason for the small sample size was that there was extreme difficulty in obtaining those who were willing to candidly discuss their experiences, especially as I was an outsider whose motives were not known to participants. Further, because each interview aimed to last exactly one hour, there was additionally a time constraint.

Another limitation was that the one who devised the interview and survey questions was also the one administering the interviews and surveys, which leaves an opening for potential bias as I was naturally looking for symptoms of TTT, even if symptoms were not overtly apparent. Additionally, despite attempts to minimize western philosophy and western psychology, I have spent most of my life in the United States and have been trained by four psychology programs that all operate off of western ideology. Creswell (2014) warns of reflexivity, in which the researcher's personal background, culture, and experiences shape the researcher's interpretation of the data.

The language barrier was another concerning limitation. Even without an interpreter, there existed much chance for linguistic confusion throughout the interviews. There was a further confounding element that participants who spoke English may have had different experiences than participants who did not speak any English, and the impact of this facet is not easily measurable. For instance, extremely religious Orthodox Jews only speak Hebrew, intentionally foregoing English. Without an interpreter, this population was inaccessible to me. As such, attempting to conduct a non-western study entirely in English is a bit of an oxymoron.

Much of the impetus for generational-focused trauma research came from the idea of the second generation: that descendants of Jews who survived the Holocaust appeared to suffer from post-traumatic symptoms as if they personally had endured the horrors of it. While the idea of the second generation would apply to Jewish refugees who fled Nazi-infested Europe to safer places, this application perhaps does not exist in Israel due to the fact that every Israeli generation since 1948 has endured at least a fleeting time of violence. The second generation of the Holocaust is simultaneously the primary generation of the modern Israeli-Palestinian Conflict. In essence, I was asking a group of people if they had been vicariously affected by ancient traumas when, in fact, they had personally dealt with rocket attacks themselves. This made it very difficult to separate the effects of TTT from their own personal trauma. Kogan (2012) argued that the modern-day Jewish population has fewer resources to deal with their perceived trauma because they were not a part of the meaning-making process for it originally; as long as members of the "first generation" are present, it is unlikely that those in the second generation will ever feel adequate enough to propose different meaning than what the first generation already affixed to the experience.

As I informed my participants about the true purpose of my research during the debriefing, I gathered many insights about my study's limitations. One participant specifically told me, "What you're studying does actually exist, but you're not going to find it with your study." She listed several reasons why she believed this, but none stronger than the fact that I had limited my search. Specifically, each of my interviews with Israelis were with nationals who were currently living in Jerusalem, and my Palestinian interviews were with Palestinians living in larger Palestinian cities (i.e., Bethlehem, Ramallah, and Jericho). According to this participant's feedback, the concept of TTT would more likely be observable in Israelis who live near the Gaza border and Palestinians who live near Israeli settlements. My pursuit was not unlike a man who goes into Chicago and determines that Illinois must not have very many cows within the state.

As such, I wish I had achieved more in-group variance. For instance, none of the Palestinians I interviewed were under "refugee" status. Interviewing five refugees and then interviewing five Ramallans would lead to very different conclusions, despite all 10 of them being Palestinian. Likewise, an Ethiopian Jew living in a settlement on Palestinian territory would likely result in different conclusions than if I were to interview a Russian Jew living in the Old City. Not only would have this likely resulted in more diverse answers regarding the political landscape, but also the religious landscape.

To that end, I wish I had asked more questions about the Temple Mount, which is perhaps closer to the heart of Abrahamic eschatology than is Gog and Magog. As previously mentioned in Chapter 1, Jews believe the messianic age will be ushered in when the Third Temple is built on the Temple Mount; until this happens, neither does the messianic age (Shenk, 2007). But the Temple Mount currently hosts the Muslims' revered al-Aqsa and the Dome of the Rock, so these structures must be removed for the Third Temple to be constructed – obviously an undertaking that is not going to happen without a literal fight. While some Jews and Palestinians may not be familiar with the religious significance of Gog and Magog, nearly all Jews and Palestinians understand the religious and political significance of the Temple Mount. I should have focused more questions on this contested land.

In hindsight, it seems I simultaneously overestimated and underestimated the impact of religion – both in a religious sense and an ethnic one. I overestimated the impact in the sense that most of the participants had fallen away from their faith. At the same time, I underestimated the impact in the sense that the most religious Jews and the most religious Muslims are guarded against secularism, therefore I was not able to represent their voices. Not only did I fail to find them, but even if I had been able to, I reiterate that I likely would not have been able to interview them because I did not have an interpreter to translate for me. As I mentioned several paragraphs ago, I limited my project to English-speakers without realizing that doing so would permeate my whole study with western bias, because it means that every participant would have been exposed to western culture and a western way of thinking about things. In fact, one of the Palestinian participants was only ever taught Arabic, but had picked up English as an additional language because he has spent the past ten years playing western video games and consequently learned the language just from his sheer exposure to western culture. (Interestingly, this participant was perhaps the best English-speaking Palestinian that I met in my entire time in the Middle East.)

The nature of western research ethics also appeared to be at odds with Middle Eastern culture, which is a culture I found to be much more informal and perhaps even adversarial to formality. In Israel especially, the zeitgeist is to not acknowledge the zeitgeist – the weight of the conflict is present, but discussions about it are usually indirect and subtle. Contrast this with the fact that I was a researcher who had to identify myself as a researcher and cite a list of rules (i.e., informed consent) prior to each interview, and it becomes easy to imagine the proverbial wall I had to build between myself and my participants (who favored informality). An anecdote worth sharing is that when I revealed myself to be a researcher trying to understand the conflict, one Israeli referred me to his friend whom he believed would be very open to talking to me as she had lived in a settlement and had experienced firsthand the ramifications of the conflict. I later met her and asked her if she would be interested in talking to me about her experiences, and she seemed to show some mild interest until I identified myself as an American researcher, to which she laughed out loud and then responded, "It's funny how you Americans always see this thing." I asked her, "Well, how do I see it?" She smirked and then dismissed me, saying, "Good luck."

This is not to say that Israelis do not have commentary on the conflict. I had many in-depth, meaningful conversations with Israelis, but many of these discussions lost a certain authenticity when I formally introduced my end purpose. I have gleaned a lot about the Israeli-Palestinian Conflict, but much of it cannot be shared in an official research capacity because these came from informal conversations in which my role as a researcher and their role as a participant were not established. I met an American journalist during my travels who succinctly explained to me, "Israelis want to provide opinions, not data."

I do not mean to imply that engaging in such ethical safeguards is erroneous. The conflict is a very sensitive issue, and any outsider who wishes to immerse himself/herself into understanding the conflict must also understand this reality. Yet, this makes it very difficult to gather data in what might be considered a "natural environment." I did not record my conversations with participants, so many of the summaries and analyses are actually just my interpretations of the conversations. As a result, the reader loses the authenticity of the interviews. This constitutes a major shortcoming – if not the most damaging shortcoming – to this study.

This is compounded with the unfortunate fact that any retrospective narrative study suffers from the limitation that interviewees are simply "remembering a memory" (Hirsch, 1997). Braga et al. (2012) note that in such instances, interviewees often only use the past as a canvas to paint the picture, but use their present feelings and attitudes as the brush strokes. Each participant here had a willingness to "paint the picture," which intrinsically eliminates a significant portion of the population who possibly have a severe form of TTT that disallows them from even talking about these traumas.

I should also note that I feel as if I was operating on bad information. Katz and Lavee noted, "The percentage of Israeli families who have suffered injury or loss, or who have close relatives or personal friends who have experienced this suffering, approaches 100%" (2004, p. 495). Katz and Lavee are not alone in ascribing to this notion as I was anecdotally informed of this several times prior to travel: When trying to find candidates for this research, I asked an Israeli professor at Tel Aviv University if he could help me identify any Israelis who had been affected by the conflict, and he responded, "It is basically everyone in Israel." This persistent idea that every Israeli and every Palestinian could point to the conflict and identify ways that their lives had been impacted by the conflict or was reeling from the effects of trauma was not indicated in my research: 11 of the 17 participants (64.7%) reported no personal trauma resulting from the conflict. This is a significant disparity and is in itself worthy of further research.

To this end, I am not confident that there truly exists "current research" on the conflict due to the nature of the ongoing development of the conflict's history: nobody can become truly versed with the context of the conflict because it is always changing. For instance, at the outset of this study, the United States had not yet recognized Jerusalem as the official capital of Israel. The December 2017 decision by U.S. President Donald Trump to move the U.S. Embassy to Jerusalem added a new chapter to the larger conflict that had not existed yet when I sought to analyze the history of the U.S.'s involvement in the Israeli-Palestinian Conflict. The very day after you become educated about the Israeli-Palestinian Conflict, you are already operating on outdated information (Cobban, 2010).

Pyramid of Psychosocial Services and
Mental Health Support Intervention

A critical observation about my study is the one-dimensional scope it provides. When I set out on this study, I assumed that Israelis and Palestinians would benefit equally from my research, and therefore I approached these two trauma-torn communities with the same aplomb that they most desperately needed to have their stories heard. However, the Inter-Agency Standing Committee (IASC) has poured itself into understanding the nuanced dynamics that face communities after a trauma manifests and have created a framework for international trauma intervention. According to their framework, I have widely missed the mark.

In recent history, when a significant disaster has struck an underdeveloped community outside of the United States, many well-meaning westerners have flocked to the affected area to offer mental health services and psychosocial resources (Watters, 2010). The IASC has identified this as a problem, namely because offering "mental health services and psychosocial resources" is the wrong order of operations, in the same way one does not subtract from a mathematical equation until the multiplication, division, and addition are all first completed. Instead, the psychosocial needs must be met before the mental health needs of a community can be addressed. The IASC developed the Psychosocial Services and Mental Health Support Intervention Pyramid to illustrate the correct order of operations for mental health professionals and laypersons alike (see Diagram 4). These guidelines were created in collaboration with several international organizations, including the World Health Organization, American Red Cross, International Organization for Migration, and several United Nations micro-departments, and was designed (and has been validated) as being both culturally responsive and mission effective (IASC, 2007).

Like any pyramid, the base is the most important part as it lays the foundation for the rest of the pyramid, which would collapse without it. The base of the Psychosocial Support Intervention Pyramid – and thus its foundation – is the layer of basic services and security.

DIAGRAM 4: IASC Pyramid of Psychosocial Services and Mental Health Support Intervention (IASC, 2007)

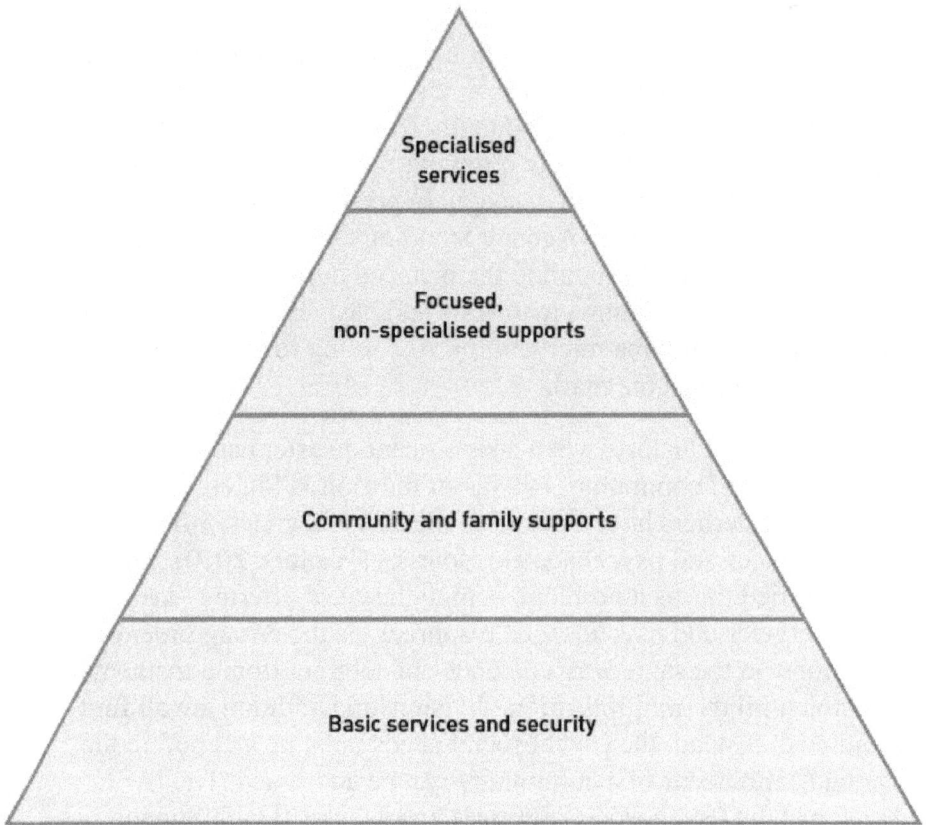

Specialised
services

Focused,
non-specialised supports

Community and family supports

Basic services and security

What this means is that the largest group of people will be arriving on-ground to the emergency area and will only be providing for the most urgent essentials. This team will find out what the basic physical needs are for the people affected by the disaster, what kind of food is needed, and what the cultural context is for that demographic (IASC, 2007). Perhaps the most startling aspect of this phase is that psychologists are not only *not needed* at this point, but they are *unwanted* because most mental health care professionals will gravitate towards exercising their expertise in mental health care which has been found to be harmful when it is used as an intervention too early in the aftermath of a disaster. By addressing the psychosocial needs of the environment, a whopping 50% of victims will be sufficiently taken care of and will not need further assistance.

On the next rung of the pyramid is the community and family support systems. At this level, community-based interventions should be used, which means that the community should be relied upon to understand the safety, survival, and community needs that will help to normalize daily life. Practically speaking, intervention teams will ideally focus on helping achieve family reunification and providing the appropriate resources to individuals so they can mourn that which they have lost. Appropriately taking care of this part of the pyramid will quell an additional 25% of people's needs, raising the total of people who no longer need assistance to 75% (IASC, 2007). At this level of intervention, mental health professionals are *still* undesired as most of the work is outside the realm of their expertise.

On the third rung of the pyramid is the focused, non-specialized support system. This is the first rung in which mental health professionals are desired, as primary mental health care is now the focus here (IASC, 2007). This means that broad counseling (such as group sessions or educational seminars) is used here. In doing this, an additional estimated 12% to 18% of victims will find themselves adequately treated and ready to function in their post-trauma lives.

The remaining 7% to 13% find themselves at the top of the pyramid, where specialized services are needed, including one-on-one counseling and addressing the specific traumatic needs of the community that has been affected (IASC, 2007). The specific needs of individuals are addressed here and are given referrals to the specialized doctors they need for recovery. This is the first level at which diagnoses should be made; never sooner.

Of interest here is that while I was in Israel and Palestine, I began to notice that my interviews with Israelis were often significantly longer than with Palestinians, and it seemed to me that Israelis had much more macro-level commentary to provide than did Palestinians. Additionally, Israelis tended to focus on the way the conflict affected Israel as a whole nation, whereas Palestinians who discussed this conflict seemed to have more to say in regards to the way the conflict affected them and their family unit individually. This is particularly surprising given that Arab culture is normally collectivistic in nature while Israel scores 54% on Hofstede's individualism dimension (Vaughn, 2010), suggesting these roles should be reversed. I was briefly tempted to conjecture that the conflict actually has a larger macro-effect on Israelis than it does Palestinians, but the IASC's pyramid provides a tenable reason for the difference: it is likely that Israelis are more poised to engage in higher-level meaning-making than their Palestinian counterparts who are perhaps still scrounging for basic services and security.

In Chapter 2, I mentioned a longitudinal study by Hobfoll et al. (2009) that determined those with more resources were more likely to achieve resilience in the face of mass casualty. In Chapter 1, I previously discussed research by Stein et al. (2013) that discussed the resiliency of one "rich" community (i.e., Otef Aza) as opposed to one "poorer" community (i.e., Sderot): those in Sderot were much less equipped to handle trauma than those in Otef Aza because of the disparity in resources available in each community. In my own study, participant Palestinian Six even spoke to this reality, stating that the conflict is exacerbated by Arabs' lack of education. This research and this anecdote certainly support IASC's position that those without basic resources may not be able to engage in meaning-making processes (IASC, 2007).

At the outset of this endeavor, I approached the Israeli-Palestinian Conflict from a purely cerebral direction, focusing on the psychological processes that affect Israelis and Palestinians. Like many other well-intentioned mental health professionals, I figured that nearly 100% of the conflict's participants would benefit from such an analysis. If the IASC is to be believed, then I have considered solutions that might actually only help 25% of the population (at best). Those who are without the practical resources to handle the trauma from the conflict – that is, namely, the Palestinians – need more than psychological understanding: they need safety, security, and support systems first. In trauma situations, mental health support is secondary to providing psychosocial services.

Recommendations

The most important value of this study can be found in its recommendations for future studies, of which there are three. The first recommendation is that the term "Israeli" and "Palestinian" not be used as the primary participant motif. These broad descriptions are too encompassing to be helpful or accurate; it would be like conducting a study on the political opinion of Americans, and placing participants from downtown Los Angeles into the same fold as those from Marfa, Texas. Future studies should refrain from clumping Tel Aviv Israelis into the same participant pool as Hebron settlement Israelis (as just one example). Likewise for Palestinians, it is problematic to place a college-educated Palestinian from Birzeit University into the same participant category as a Palestinian who lives under Hamas leadership in Gaza. Surprisingly, most studies do not attempt to differentiate between the types of backgrounds of Israelis and Palestinians, and this can cause clumsy results. In the future, it would be especially helpful to distinguish Israelis and Palestinians who live near/in settlements, who have a college education, and who have formal military experience. Not only would this create more specificity of who exactly is being evaluated in a particular study, but it could help pave the way to an "Israeli Psychology" or "Palestinian Psychology" in the same vein as "Filipino Psychology," which is an indigenous psychology birthed by Virgilio Enriquez, who argued that western psychology tenets did not apply to his Filipino culture. In response, Enriquez created "Sikolohiyang Pilipino" to become a psychological framework unique to the Philippines that rejected many of the assumptions that had driven western psychology (Pe-Pau & Protacio-Marcelino, 2000).

The second recommendation is that an instrument be developed to more accurately assess TTT. Such an instrument would benefit from exploring the topic of resiliency to allow room for discussion on post-traumatic growth. Further, early studies on TTT also indicate that those who suffer from TTT actually relive their parents' trauma at the same age as their parents did (Kellerman, 2001), so adding questions about onset of TTT and/or traditional trauma may help to detect patterns in different families or populations.

144

But most importantly, this instrument ought to more deeply consider the physical manifestations of trauma and consider survivors' inhibition processes. While questions about night terrors and anxiety and other psychologically-based symptoms are relevant, there is a lot of value in considering the other manifestations of trauma, too. Brown (2017) examined TTT in indigenous aboriginal populations in Australia and found that TTT resulted in negative behavioral patterns that included alcoholism, substance abuse, domestic violence, and high rates of incarceration. Similarly, most of my questions were hyper-focused on the mental effects of trauma, but I heard several instances of anecdotal evidence during my trip that those who have endured the most extreme kinds of trauma also end up having physical ailments like diabetes, ulcers, cancer, and poor heart health. I was unprepared to field questions about this manifestation, and I regret not being able to consider the possibility that those who are not "afraid" of trauma in the traditional western sense might be experiencing negative effects in other physical areas of their life. Queries about such physical manifestations could easily be added to the assessing questionnaire.

To this end, the word "trauma" needs to be better operationalized across cultures; there is a difference between losing a limb versus witnessing something horrific. Yet, the former is more often the sole definition for Israelis and Palestinians, while the latter is a more frequent definition for westerners. If I could choose which of my takeaways would be given most consideration in a future study, it is this: do not overlook the negative physical effects of trauma. TTT will never be fully understood until the physiological consequences are examined.

Finally, based on the IASC (2007) Psychosocial Services and Mental Health Support Intervention Pyramid, future studies may provide more meaningful insight by simply analyzing the psychosocial gaps that exist collectively and individually for Israelis and Palestinians. This can be done by either including psychosocial questions on the questionnaire or by having such information about the specific region's population prior to data collection. It may be the case that addressing the underlying psychological processes of this conflict is an ointment that only covers a quarter of the wound. It is perhaps true that Israelis would better thrive if their stories were heard and their psychological processes were understood; after all, most Israelis have their needs met on the bottom two foundational rungs of the Psychosocial Services and Mental Health Support Intervention Pyramid. However, this does not seem to be the case for Palestinians who largely are not even on a level where their mental health is a priority; most are just trying to survive. Most Israelis are in position to evaluate the conflict and can engage in meaning-making processes, whereas most Palestinians just want a safe place to sleep. Researchers should stop treating these two populations as if they are living the same realities just because they are living the same conflict.

Conclusion

Two generations later, the Holocaust's sting is still felt: the tragedy has been absorbed into the identity of survivors' descendants, while Palestinians feel as if the event is being wielded against them as potential perpetrators of a second Shoah. As a rookie researcher, I attempted to bring a semblance of sense to all of the gravitas of the resultant conflict. Within just a few interviews into my data collection, I recognized that the scope of my project was much too broad, and research about the Israeli-Palestinian Conflict must further break down the nuances of its different elements. It was a mistake to attempt to represent *all* Israelis or *all* Palestinians in one study. It is arrogant to assume "trauma" means the same thing in the Middle East as it does in the western world. No single study can cover "Transgenerational Trauma Transmission in the Israeli-Palestinian Conflict"; a more accurate title for what I have studied is perhaps "Concepts of Trauma in Jerusalem-based Jews and Bethlehem-/Ramallah-/Jericho-based Palestinians," and even with this specific focus, I barely scratched the surface of what might be found.

The people that I interviewed had different psychological processes than most Americans I know: I found that Israelis and Palestinians are not generally afraid of death. When I consider why this is, I walk away with the conclusion that Israelis and especially Palestinians are trying to work towards something bigger than themselves; their life and death is but a chapter of Jewish and Arab history. I wish for the reader to walk away with a better understanding of their role in that history, too. In Chapter 2, commentary from

146

Sabbah (2015) emphasized that religion and military should never operate together, but as both Israeli and Palestinian government mandate special permissions to visit specific places that are holy to Jews and Muslims, this is what has been achieved. However, Sabbah also notes that the good news is that for as much as religion is a confounding variable in this conflict, it can also be a vessel to peace and reconciliation. Both religions (i.e., Judaism and Islam) revere God as supreme and humans as fallible, which should be a foothold when handling religious discussions of the topic. Sabbah encourages greater influence from the Council of Religious Institutions in the Holy Land, a 2002 council designed to incite dialogue (as opposed to violence) across religious persons.

Golan (2015b) has outlined specific steps that the United States are burdened to take in order to become better mediators in the conflict. The UN Security Council Resolution 446 states that "settlements have no legal validity and constitute a serious obstruction to achieving a comprehensive, just, and lasting peace in the Middle East." This resolution was passed in 1979, and reaffirmed in 1980, 2002, 2003, 2008, and 2016, but no practical efforts have been proposed by the United States or any members of the UN. The United States – which is no stranger to meddling in Middle Eastern politics – often cites Israel's "right to defend" as the reason why settlements must be allowed (Jhally, Alper, & Earp, 2016), and while there is merit to this argument in militarily strategic places like the Golan Heights or religiously significant places like Hebron, there is no clear delineation between areas that have this level of significance and those that do not.

As such, Resolution 446 is just as impactful as anyone who simply wishes for peace in the Middle East without actually attempting to understand its nuances. In the past, the role of the United States has been confined to mediating or policing the conflict. Instead, perhaps the Israeli-Palestinian Conflict should be approached like a humanitarian issue rather than a political foreign diplomacy issue.

I leave the reader with a quote from a young Israeli boy as documented in Shapiro and Goldberg's 2002 documentary, <u>Promises</u>: "In war, both sides suffer. Maybe there's a winner, but what's a 'winner?' People on both sides die. Both sides lose."

Acknowledgements

First and foremost, I thank the God of Abraham, Isaac, and Jacob, who called me to consider His precious people in the Holy Land, and then allowed me to fulfill this call. I also extend special appreciation to my chair, Dr. Giddie, whom I lied to when I told him that I would be the easiest student he's ever taken on in his life. Thank you to Jacob Carlson, whose historical expertise helped me to appropriately reframe the context of the Israeli-Palestinian Conflict. Thank you to Dr. Karen Brown for stepping in as an editor on short notice. Special thanks also go to the Ruas twins, who were unexpected, unparalleled resources while in (and after) Israel and Palestine. Thank you to my family who pushed me through the trials that occurred during this four-year-plus endeavor, and especially Joanna, who not only helped me find scholarly sources and was a final editor to this project, but was also of critical value as she provided significant encouragement ($p<.0001$), was extremely reliable ($\alpha = .999$), and is the most positive Pearson correlation coefficient I have ever discovered.

Abusoboh, A. (2016). Post-traumatic stress disorder scale and Palestinian trauma. *Pangaea Journal, 7*. Retrieved from http://sites.stedwards.edu/pangaea/post-traumatic-stress-disorder-scale-and-palestinian-trauma/.

Al Husseini, J., Bocco, R., Brunner, M., & Bühler, C. (2007, September). *The legal status of the Palestinian refugees in the Near East: Formal aspects and perceptions.* Workshop presented at From Exodus to Exile: Palestinian Lives in the Levant, Bergen, Norway. Retrieved from https://www.cmi.no/file/?120.

Al-Jazeera (2018, 30 Dec.) The events that shook the Palestinian territories in 2018. *Al-Jazeera.* Retrieved from https://www.aljazeera.com/news/2018/12/events-shook-palestinian-territories-2018-181228140137550.html.

Alexander, J. C., Eyerman, R., & Giesen, B. (2004). *Cultural trauma and collective identity.* Berkeley, CA: University of California Press.

Altawil, M., Nel, P.W., Asker, A., Samara, M., & Harrold, D. (2008). The effects of chronic war trauma among Palestinian children. In M. Parsons (Ed.), *Children: The invisible victims of war: An interdisciplinary study.* Peterborough, England: DSM Technical Publications Ltd.

Arikan, K., Uysal, O., & Cetin, G. (1999). Public awareness of the effectiveness of psychiatric treatment may reduce stigma. *The Israel Journal of Psychiatry and Related Sciences, 36*(2), 95-99.

Aronson, I.M. (1980). Geographical and socioeconomic factors in the 1881 anti-Jewish pogroms in Russia. *The Russian Review, 39*(1), 18-31.

Artzi-Medvedik, R., Chertok, I. R. A., & Romem, Y. (2012). Nurses' attitudes towards breastfeeding among women with schizophrenia in southern Israel. *Journal of Psychiatric and Mental Health Nursing, 19*(8), 702-708.

Astashkevich, I. (2018). *Gendered Violence: Jewish Women in the Pogroms of 1917 to 1921* (pp. 18-37). Boston, MA: Academic Studies Press.

Atkinson, J., Nelson, J., Brooks, R., Atkinson, C., & Ryan, K. (2014). Addressing individual and community transgenerational trauma. In P. Dudgeon, H. Milroy, & R. Walker, (Eds.). *Working together: Aboriginal and Torres Strait Islander mental health and well-being principles and practice* (2nd ed.) (pp. 289-306). Commonwealth of Australia.

Auerhahn, N.C. & Laub, D. (1998). Intergenerational memory of the Holocaust. In Y. Danieli (Ed.), *International Handbook of Multigenerational Legacies of Trauma* (pp. 21-41). New York, NY: Plenum Press.

Aupperle, R. L. (2018). Evidence over dogma: Embracing an expanding repertoire of PTSD treatment options. *The American Journal of Psychiatry, 175*(10), 927-928.

Ayer, L., Venkatesh, B., Stewart, R., Mandel, D., Stein, B., & Schoenbaum, M. (2015). Psychological aspects of the Israeli-Palestinian conflict: A systematic review. *Trauma, Violence, & Abuse.* Retrieved from https://www.ncbi.nlm.nih.gov/pubmed/26511933.

Aziza, S. (2017, Dec. 8). Palestine's First Intifada is still a model for grassroots resistance. *The Nation.* Retrieved from https://www.thenation.com/article/palestines-first-intifada-is-still-a-model-for-grassroots-resistance/.

Bar-Tal, D., & Halperin, E. (2014). Societal beliefs and emotions as socio-psychological barriers to peaceful conflict resolution. *Palestine-Israel Journal of Politics, Economics & Culture, 19*(3), 18-27.

Bartová, B. (2016). The memory of Topoľčany: the relationship of the Jewish inhabitants of Topoľčany after the tragedy of the "Topoľčany pogrom." *Journal of Modern Jewish Studies, 15*(3), 520-525.

Bass, G.J. (2010, Mar. 31). When Israel and France broke up. *The New York Times.* Retrieved from https://www.nytimes.com/2010/04/01/opinion/01bass.html.

BBC News (2018, November 13). Israel-Gaza violence erupts after covert op killings. *BBC News.* Retrieved from https://www.bbc.com/news/world-middle-east-46185653.

Ben-Dror, E., & Ziedler, A. (2015). Israel, Jordan, and their efforts to frustrate the United Nations resolutions to internationalise Jerusalem. *Diplomacy & Statecraft, 26*(1), 636-658.

Berry, J.W., Poortinga, Y.H., Bruegelmans, S.M., Chasiotis, A., & Sam, D.L. (2011). *Cross-cultural psychology: Research and applications* (3rd ed.). Cambridge, UK: Cambridge University Press.

Birnbaum, A. (2008). Collective trauma and post-traumatic symptoms in the biblical narrative of ancient Israel. *Journal of Mental Health, Religion & Culture, 11*(5), 533-546.

Bisel, R.S., & Ford, D.J. (2008). Diagnosing pathogenic eschatology. *Communication Studies, 59*(4), 340-354.

Braga, L.L., Mello, M.F., & Fiks, J.P. (2012). Transgenerational transmission of trauma and resilience: A qualitative study with Brazilian offspring of Holocaust survivors. *BMC Psychiatry, 12,* 134.

Braverman, E. (2017, Nov. 11). Father Patrick Desbois: One man's fight to uncover the Holocaust. *Aish HaTorah.* Retrieved from https://www.aish.com/jw/s/Father-Patrick-Desbois-One-Mans-Fight-to-Uncover-the-Holocaust.html.

Brown, K.B. (2017*). A phenomenological study to explore transgenerational trauma: An Australian aboriginal perspective* (Unpublished doctoral dissertation). The Chicago School of Professional Psychology, Chicago, Illinois.

Brueggemann, W. (2015). *Chosen? Reading the Bible amid the Israeli-Palestinian conflict.* Louisville, KY: Westminster John Knox Press.

Brustein, W. I. (2003). *Roots of hate: Anti-Semitism in Europe before the Holocaust.* Cambridge, UK: Cambridge University Press.

Bulut, U. (2017, Sep. 8). Turkey's genocide denial: Four narratives. *The Armenian Weekly.* Retrieved from https://www.meforum.org/articles/2017/turkeys-genocide-denial-four-narratives.

Butler, C. (2001). *A world war against terrorism.* London, England: Lancet.

Canetti, D., Kimhi, S., Hanoun, R., Rocha, G.A., Galea, S., & Morgan, C.A. (2016). How personality affects vulnerability among Israelis and Palestinians following the 2009 Gaza conflict. *Public Library of Science ONE, 11*(7), 1-14.

CBN Israel (2017, May 23). *In Our Hands: The Battle for Jerusalem* [Documentary]. USA: Christian Broadcasting Network.

Cepoi, E. (2013). The origins of Hamas: An offshoot of Muslim brotherhood, or a result of the PLO's moral corruption? *Scientific Research & Education in the Air Force, 1*(1), 159-169.

Ciarrocchi, J.W. (1995). *The doubting disease: Help for scrupulosity and religious compulsions.* Mahwah, NJ: Paulist Press.

Clinton, M. (2013, June 23). Jerusalem's Eastern Gate has been closed – Messiah to come and open it. *Before It's News.* Retrieved from https://beforeitsnews.com/v3/prophecy/2013/2450730.html.

Clinton, W.J. (2000, July 25). *President William J. Clinton statement of the Middle East peace talks at Camp David* [Transcript]. Retrieved from http://avalon.law.yale.edu/21st_century/mid027.asp.

Cobban, H. (2010). Palestinian history. *Journal of Palestine Studies, 39*(4), 73-75.

Cole, M., & Hatano, G. (2010). Cultural-historical activity theory: Integrating phylogeny, cultural history. In S. Kitayama & D. Cohen, *Handbook of cultural psychology* (pp. 109-135). New York, NY: The Guilford Press.

Cone, J.D., & Foster, S.L. (2006). *Dissertations and theses from start to finish* (2nd ed.). Washington, DC: American Psychological Association.

Courtois, C.A. (2004). Complex trauma, complex reactions: Assessment and treatment. *Psychotherapy: Theory, Research, Practice, Training, 41*(4), 412-425.

Creswell, J.W. (2013). *Qualitative inquiry and research design: Choosing among five approaches* (3rd ed.). Thousand Oaks, CA: SAGE.

Creswell, J.W. (2014). *Research design: Qualitative, quantitative, and mixed methods approaches* (4th ed.). Thousand Oaks, CA: SAGE.

Dardas, L. A., & Simmons, L. A. (2015). The stigma of mental illness in Arab families: a concept analysis. *Journal of Psychiatric and Mental Health Nursing, 22*(9), 668-679.

De Girolamo, G. & McFarlane, A.C. (1996). The Epidemiology of PTSD: A comprehensive review of the international literature. In A.J. Marcella, M.J. Friedman, E.T. Gerry, & R.M. Scurfield (Eds.), *Ethnocultural aspects of posttraumatic stress disorder: Issues, research, & clinical applications* (pp. 33-85). Washington, DC: American Psychological Association.

Denham, A. R. (2008). Rethinking historical trauma: Narratives of resilience. *Transcultural Psychology, 45*(3), 391-414.

Desbois, P. (2009). *The Holocaust by bullets: A priest's journey to uncover the truth behind the murder of 1.5 million Jews.* London, England: St. Martin's Press.

Dias, B.G., & Ressler, K.J. (2014). Parental olfactory experience influences behavior and neural structure in subsequent generations. *Nature Neuroscience, 17*(1), 89-96.

Dickstein, B.D., Schorr, Y., Stein, N., Krantz, L.H., Solomon, Z., & Litz, B. (2011). Coping and mental health outcomes among Israelis living with the chronic threat of terrorism. *Psychological Trauma: Theory, Research, Practice, and Policy, 4*(4), 392-399.

Difference Between (2017, September 27). Difference between Hamas and Hezbollah. *Difference Between.* Retrieved from http://www.differencebetween.net/miscellaneous/politics/difference-between-hamas-and-hezbollah/.

Dittmer, J. (2007). Of Gog and Magog: The geopolitical visions of Jack Chick and premillennial dispensationalism. *ACME: An International Journal for Critical Geographies, 6*(2), 278-303.

Dudgeon, P., Wright, M., Paradies, Y., Garvey, D., & Walker, I. (2014). Aboriginal social, cultural, and historical contexts. In P. Dudgeon, H. Milroy, and R. Walker (Eds.). Working together: Aboriginal and Torres Strait Islander mental health and well-being principles and practice (2nd ed.) (pp. 3-24). Commonwealth of Australia.

Duran, E., & Duran, B. (1995). *Native American post-colonial psychology.* Albany, NY: State University of New York Press.

Ellis, T.J., & Levy, Y. (2009). Towards a guide for novice researchers on research methodology: Review and proposed methods. *Issues in Informing Science and Information Technology, 6*(1), 323-337.

Elman, M.F. (2016). Jerusalem studies: The state of the field. *Israel Studies, 21*(3), 221-241.

Fail, H., Thompson, J., & Walker, G. (2004). Belonging, identity, and third culture kids: Life histories of former international school students. *Journal of Research in International Education, 3*(3), 319-338.

Fetterman, D. M. (2010). *Ethnography: Step by step* (3rd ed.). Newbury Park, CA: SAGE Publications, Inc.

Ferré, F. (1970). The definition of religion. *Journal of the American Academy of Religion, 38*(1), 3-16.

Films for Action (2009). *Life in Occupied Palestine* [Video file]. Lawrence, KS: Films for Action. Retrieved from https://www.filmsforaction.org/watch/life-in-occupied-palestine/.

Fontaine, J.R.J. (2011). A fourfold conceptual framework for cultural and cross-cultural psychology: relativism, construct universalism, repertoire universalism and absolutism. In Van de Vijver, F.J. R., Chasiotis, A. & Breugelmans, S. M. (Eds.), *Fundamental questions in cross-cultural psychology* (pp. 165-189). New York, NY: Cambridge University Press.

Frantzman, S.J., & Kark, R. (2013). The Muslim settlement of late Ottoman and mandatory Palestine: Comparison with Jewish settlement patterns. *Digest of Middle East Studies, 22*(1), 74-93.

Friedman, E. (2016). Recognition gaps in the Israeli-Palestinian conflict: The people-state and self-other axes. *Journal of Language and Politics, 15*(2), 193-214.

Geertz, C. (1973). *The interpretation of cultures*. New York, NY: Basic Books.

Geist, D. (2012). *I am Danger; I am Prisoner*. Lake Villa, IL: Burning Bridge Publishing.

Geist, D. (2016). *Mister master exacerbation: My obsessive quest to uncover the final compulsion, and how my porn use got me fired from work, kicked out of school, banned from my field, separated from my wife, and warped me into an animal-abuser, a fugitive, and an all-around villain*. Round Lake Beach, IL: Burning Bridge Publishing.

Gleis, J.L., & Berti, B. (2012). *Hezbollah and Hamas: A comparative study*. Baltimore, MD: John Hopkins University Press.

Golan, G. (2015a). The Israeli-Palestinian conflict: Lessons for a breakthrough. *Middle East Policy, 22*(3), 100-108.

Golan, G. (2015b). Suggestions for American mediation of the Israeli-Palestinian conflict. *Palestine-Israel Journal of Politics, Economics & Culture, 20*(2-3), 46-50.

Gomby, R. (2017, Aug. 8). The story behind Jerusalem's sealed Golden Gate. *Culture Trip*. Retrieved from https://theculturetrip.com/middle-east/israel/articles/the-story-behind-jerusalems-sealed-golden-gate/.

155

Goodwin, J. (2012). Is religious extremism a major cause of terrorism? NO: 'Religious terrorism' as ideology. In Jackson, R. & Sinclair, S. (Eds), *Contemporary Debates on Terrorism*. Abingdon, UK: Taylor & Francis.

Got Questions (2018). What is the significance of the Eastern Gate of Jerusalem? *GotQuestions.org*. Retrieved from https://www.gotquestions.org/eastern-gate-Jerusalem.html.

Graham, C. & Chattopadhyay, S. (2009). Well-being and public attitudes in Afghanistan: Some insights from the economics of happiness. *World Economics, 10*(3), 105-146.

Gross, Z., & Gamal, E. (2014). How Muslim Arab-Israeli teachers conceptualize the Israeli-Arab conflict in class. *Studies in Philosophy & Education, 33*(1), 267-281.

Gunter, R.J. (2015, Apr. 17). Where in the world is Tarshish? *The Christian Pulse.* Retrieved from http://thechristianpulse.com/2015/04/17/where-in-the-world-is-tarshish/.

Haj, D.S. (2015). *Post-traumatic stress disorder among Arabs: The effects of culture on etiology and symptoms* (Unpublished doctoral dissertation). The Chicago School of Professional Psychology, Chicago, Illinois.

Haughey, N. (2006, Feb. 2). Israel delays transfer of €37m in tax rebates to Palestinians. *Irish Times*. Retrieved from https://www.irishtimes.com/news/israel-delays-transfer-of-37m-in-tax-rebates-to-palestinians-1.1009825.

Haushofer, J., Biletzki, A., & Kanwisher, N. (2010). Both sides retaliate in the Israeli-Palestinian conflict. *Proceedings of the National Academy of Sciences, 107*(42), 17927-17932.

Heim, L., & Schaal, S. (2014). Rates and predictors of mental stress in Rwanda: Investigating the impact of gender, persecution, readiness to reconcile and religiosity via a structural equation model. *International Journal of Mental Health Systems, 8*(1), 1-9.

Herman, J. (2012). CPTSD is a distinct entity: Comment on Resick et al. (2012). *Journal of Traumatic Stress, 25*(3), 256-257.

Hirsch, M. (1997). *Family frames: Photography, narrative, and postmemory.* Cambridge, MA: Harvard University Press.

Hirsch, M. (2008). The generation of postmemory. *Poetics Today, 29*(1), 103−28.

Hobfoll, S. E., Palmieri, P. A., Johnson, R. J., Canetti-Nisim, D., Hall, B. J., & Galea, S. (2009). Trajectories of resilience, resistance, and distress during ongoing terrorism: The case of Jews and Arabs in Israel. *Journal of Consulting and Clinical Psychology, 77*(1), 138-148.

Holloway, J. (2015). Sealing future geographies: Religious prophecy and the case of Joanna Southcott. *Transactions of the Institute of British Geographers, 40*(2), 180-191.

Honneth, A. (1996). *The struggle for recognition: The moral grammar of social conflicts.* Cambridge: Polity Press.

Hugman, R., Pittaway, E., & Bartolomei, L. (2011). When 'do no harm' is not enough: The ethics of research with refugees and other vulnerable groups. *British Journal of Social Work, 41*(7), 1271-1287.

Huppert, J.D., Siev, J., & Kushner, E.S. (2007). When religion and obsessive-compulsive disorder collide: Treating scrupulosity in ultra-Orthodox Jews. *Journal of Clinical Psychology, 63*(10), 925-941.

Inter-Agency Standing Committee (IASC) (2007). IASC guidelines on mental health and psychosocial support in emergency settings. Geneva: IASC.

Iliceto, P., Candilera, G., Funaro, D., Pompili, M., Kaplan, K. J., & Markus-Kaplan, M. (2011). Hopelessness, temperament, anger and interpersonal relationships in Holocaust (Shoah) survivors' grandchildren. *Journal of Religious Health, 50*(1), 321-329.

Isaac, J. (2017). Jewish settlements in the Israeli occupied state of Palestine: Undermining authentic resolution of the Israeli-Palestinian Conflict. *Palestine-Israel Journal of Politics, Economics, and Culture, 22*(2-3), 85-91.

Israel Ministry of Foreign Affairs (2004, Mar. 22). Ahmed Yassin, leader of Hamas terrorist organization. *Israel Ministry of Foreign Affairs.* Retrieved from http://www.mfa.gov.il/mfa/foreignpolicy/terrorism/palestinian/pages/ahmed%20yas sin.aspx.

Jhally, S., Alper, L., & Earp, J. (Producers). (2016). *The Occupation of the American Mind* [Motion picture]. Northampton, MA: Media Education Foundation.

Johnson, D.A. (2017). Offensive counterintelligence: Using psychology to sabotage social bonds in terrorist organizations. In C. E. Stout (Ed.), *Terrorism, Political Violence, and Extremism: New Psychology to Understand, Face, and Defuse the Threat* (pp. 175-198). Santa Barbara, CA: Praeger.

Jones, D. (2016, September). Untying the hardest knots. *British Psychological Society, 29*(9), 690-694.

Kane, J.N., & Podell, J. (2008). *Facts about the presidents* (8th ed.). New York, NY: H.W. Wilson.

Katz, R., & Lavee, Y. (2004). Families in Israel. In B. N. Adams & J. Trost (Eds.), *Handbook of world families* (pp. 486-506). Thousand Oaks, California: Sage Publication.

Kellerman, N.P.F. (2001). Psychopathology in children of Holocaust survivors: A review of the research literature. *The Israel Journal of Psychiatry and Related Sciences, 38*(1), 36-46.

Keret, E. (2016, June 24). I'm not anti-Israel, I'm ambi-Israel. *The New York Times.* Retrieved from http://www.nytimes.com/2016/06/25/opinion/im-not-anti-israel-im-ambi-israel.html.

Kifner, J. (2007, Nov. 6). Armenian genocide of 1915: An overview. *The New York Times.* Retrieved from https://archive.nytimes.com/www.nytimes.com/ref/timestopics/topics_armeniangenocide.html?mcubz=1.

Kim, J. (2016). *Understanding narrative inquiry: The crafting and analysis of stories as research.* Thousand Oaks, CA: SAGE Publications, Inc.

Koenig, H.G., Perno, K., & Hamilton, T. (2017). The spiritual history in outpatient practice: Attitudes and practices of health professionals in the Adventist Health System. *BMC Medical Education, 17*(1), 1-12.

Kogan, I. (2012). The second generation in the shadow of terror. In M. G. Fromm (Ed.), *Lost in transmission: Studies of trauma across generations* (pp. 5-20). London: Karnac Publishing.

Kressel, N.J. (2007). Mass hatred in the Muslim and Arab world: The neglected problem of anti-Semitism. *International Journal of Applied Psychoanalytic Studies, 4*(3), 197-215.

Kuang, X. (2016). *Xunzi: The complete text* (E.L. Hutton, Trans.). Princeton, NJ: Princeton University Press. (Original work published 3rd Century B.C.)

LaCapra, D. (2001). *Writing history, writing trauma.* Baltimore, MD: John Hopkins University Press.

Laufer, A., & Solomon, Z. (2006). Posttraumatic symptoms and posttraumatic growth among Israeli youth exposed to terror incidents. *Journal of Social and Clinical Psychology, 25*(4), 429-447.

Leiken, R.S. (2005, July/August). Europe's angry Muslims. *Foreign Affairs.* Retrieved from https://www.foreignaffairs.com/articles/europe/2005-07-01/europes-angry-muslims.

Lewis, M. (2016). *The undoing project: A friendship that changed our minds.* New York City, NY: W.W. Norton & Company.

Lipstadt, D. (1993). *Denying the Holocaust: The growing assault on truth and memory.* New York, NY: The Free Press.

Loftus, E.F. (2007). A history of psychology in autobiography. In G. Lindzey & W.M. Runyan (Eds.), *A history of psychology in autobiography, Vol. IX* (pp. 199-227). Washington, DC, US: American Psychological Association.

Lustick, I. (1988). *For the land and the Lord: Jewish fundamentalism in Israel.* New York City, NY: Council on Foreign Relations, Inc.

Magdalene Publishing (2018). Jerusalem's Golden Gate history and prophecy. *Magdalene Publishing*. Retrieved from http://www.magdalenepublishing.org/blog/jerusalems-golden-gate-history-prophecy/.

Marsella, A.J. (2013, December). All psychologies are indigenous psychologies: Reflections on psychology in a global era. *Psychology International*. Retrieved from http://www.apa.org/international/pi/2013/12/reflections.aspx.

Maxwell, J. (2004). *Conceptual framework: What do you think is going on?* Sage Publications.

McCallister, B., & Schmid, A.P. (2013). Theories of terrorism. In A.P. Schmid (Ed.), *The Routledge Handbook of Terrorism Research*. Abingdon, UK: Taylor & Francis.

McNally, D. (2014). *Transgenerational trauma: Dealing with the past in Northern Ireland*. Retrieved from http://www.wavetraumacentre.org.uk/uploads/pdf/1404220890--100105-WAVE-transgen-report.pdf.

Medzini, A. (2012). The war of the maps: The political use of maps and atlases to shape national consciousness – Israel versus the Palestinian Authority. In K.C. Koutsopoulos (Ed.), *European Journal of Geography, 3*(1), 23-40.

Merrick, J., Kandel, I., & Omar, H.A. (2013). *Children, Violence and Bullying: International Perspectives*. Hauppauge, New York: Nova Science Publishers, Inc.

Miller, K.E., & Rasco, L.M. (2004). An ecological framework for addressing the mental health needs of refugee communities. In K.E. Miller & L.M. Rasco (Eds.), *The mental health of refugees: Ecological approaches to healing and adaptation* (pp. 1-64). Mah Wah, NJ: Lawrence Erlbaum Associates, Publishers.

Mock, C., Joshipura, M., Arreola-Risa, C., & Quansah, R. (2012). An estimate of the number of lives that could be saved through improvements in trauma care globally. *World Journal of Surgery, 36*(1), 959-963.

Moghaddam, F. (2005). The staircase to terrorism: A psychological exploration. *American Psychologist, 60*(2), 161-169.

Mollica, R.F., Caspi, Y., Bollini, P., Truong, T., Tor, S., & LaVelle, J. (1992). The Harvard Trauma Questionnaire. *Journal of Nervous & Mental Disease, 80*(2), 111-116.

Molloy, M. (2013). *Experiencing the world's religions* (6th ed.). New York City, NY: McGraw Hill Higher Education.

Morgenstern, J. (1929). The gates of righteousness. *Hebrew Union College Annual, 6*, 1-37.

Munroe, A., & Moghaddam, F.M. (2012). Is religious extremism a major cause of terrorism? YES: Religious extremism as a major cause of terrorism. In Jackson, R. & Sinclair, S. (Eds.), *Contemporary Debates on Terrorism*. Abingdon, UK: Taylor & Francis.

159

Murray, J.A., & O'Driscoll, A. (1997). Messianic eschatology: Some redemptive reflections on marketing and the benefits of a process approach. *European Journal of Marketing, 31*(9-10), 706-719.

Nadan, Y., & Ben-Ari, A. (2015). Social work education in the context of armed political conflict: An Israeli perspective. *British Journal of Social Work, 45*(1), 1734-1749.

Nets-Zehngut, R. (2014). The Israeli and Palestinian collective memories of their conflict: Determinants, characteristics, and implications. *The Brown Journal of World Affairs, 20*(2), 103-121.

Obeidi, A. (2014). Special issue: The Israeli-Palestinian and related conflicts. *Group Decis Negot, 23*(1), 1241-1243.

Omeish, A., & Omeish, S. (Producers). (2006*). Occupation 101: Voices of the Silenced Majority* [Documentary]. Los Angeles, CA: Trip'ol'ii Productions.

Osman, K. (2000, August 1-15). Palestinians want new intifada as Camp David II ends without deal after 15 days. *Crescent International.*

Pe-Pau, R., & Protacio-Marcelino, E.A. (2000). Sikolohiyang Pilipino (Filipino psychology): A legacy of Virgilio G. Enriquez. *Asian Journal of Social Psychology, 3*(1), 49-71.

Pescosolido, B., Medina, T., Martin, J., & Long, J. (2013). The "backbone" of stigma: Identifying the global core of public prejudice associated with mental illness. *American Journal of Public Health*, e1-e8.

Piven, J.S. (2017). Psychological, theological, and thanatological aspects of suicide terrorism. In C. E. Stout (Ed.), *Terrorism, Political Violence, and Extremism: New Psychology to Understand, Face, and Defuse the Threat* (pp. 79-102). Santa Barbara, CA: Praeger.

Putra, I. E., & Sukabdi, Z. A. (2014). Can Islamic fundamentalism relate to nonviolent support? The role of certain conditions in moderating the effect of Islamic fundamentalism on supporting acts of terrorism. *Peace and Conflict: Journal of Peace Psychology, 20*(4), 583-589.

Ramsbotham, O., Woodhouse, T., & Miall, H. (2011). *Contemporary conflict resolution* (3rd ed.). Cambridge, UK: Polity.

Regnerus, M.D., & Uecker, J.E. (2007). Religious influences on sensitive self-reported behaviors: The product of social desirability, deceit, or embarrassment? *Sociology of Religion, 68*(2), 145-163.

Republic of Turkey (2011). The Armenian allegation of genocide: The issue and the facts. eVisa. *Republic of Turkey Ministry of Foreign Affairs*. Retrieved from http://www.mfa.gov.tr/the-armenian-allegation-of-genocide-the-issue-and-the-facts.en.mfa.

Reynolds, E. H., & Wilson, J. V. K. (2012). Obsessive compulsive disorder and psychopathic behaviour in Babylon. *Journal of Neurology and Neurosurgical Psychiatry, 83*(1), 199-201.

Robinson, G.E. (1997). *Building a Palestinian state: The incomplete revolution.* Bloomington, IN: Indiana University Press.

Robinson, G.E. (2007). The Palestinian Hamas: Vision, violence, and coexistence. *Middle East Policy, 14*(1), 163-166.

Rosenberg, J. C. (2008). *Epicenter 2.0: Why the Current Rumblings in the Middle East Will Change Your Future.* Carol Stream, IL: Tyndale House Publishers, Inc.

Rydelnik, M. (2007). *Understanding the Arab-Israeli conflict: What the headlines haven't told you.* Chicago, IL: Moody Publishers.

Sabatinelli, G., Pace-Shanklin, S., Riccardo, F., & Shahin, Y. (2009). Palestinian refugees outside the occupied Palestinian territory. *The Lancet, 373*(1), 1063-1065.

Sabbah, M. (2015). Religion and the Palestinian-Israeli conflict. *Palestine-Israel Journal of Politics, Economics, and Culture, 20-21*(41).

Sabella, B. (2019). Is the two-state solution feasible? *Palestine-Israel Journal, 24*(1), 80-84.

Saldaña, J. (2016). *The coding manual for qualitative research* (3rd ed.). London: SAGE Publishing.

Saleem, M., & Anderson, C. A. (2013). Arabs as terrorists: Effects of stereotypes within violent contexts on attitudes, perceptions, and affect. *Psychology of Violence, 3*(1), 84-99.

Scham, P. (2015). Perceptions of anti-Semitism in the Israeli-Palestinian conflict. *Palestine-Israel Journal of Politics, Economics, and Culture, 20*(4) & *21*(1), 114-120.

Schori-Eyal, N., Halperin, E., & Bar-Tal, D. (2014). Three layers of collective victimhood: Effects of multileveled victimhood on intergroup conflicts in the Israeli-Arab context. *Journal of Applied Social Psychology, 44*(1), 778-794.

Schwanitz, W.G. (2018). A Jewish national home: 100 years on the "Ottoman Balfour Declaration." *Middle East Quarterly, 25*(1), 1-8.

Seita, A., & Shaikh, I. A. (2013). Worsening plight of Palestinian refugees in Syria. *The Lancet, 382*, 680.

Sen, S. (2015). "It's *nakba*, not a party": Re-Stating the (Continued) Legacy of the Oslo Accords. *Arab Studies Quarterly, 37*(2), 161-176.

Shapiro, J., & Goldberg, B.Z. (Producers). (2002, March 15). *Promises* [Documentary]. USA: New Yorker Video.

Shenk, D.W. (2009). Muslims and Christians: Eschatology and mission. *International Bulletin of Missionary Research, 33*(3), 120-123.

Sinclair, M. (2007, June). Editorial: A guide to understanding theoretical and conceptual frameworks. *Evidence-Based Midwifery.*

Smith, J.A., Flowers, P., & Larkin, M. (2009). *Interpretative phenomenological analysis: Theory, method, and research.* London: SAGE Publications, Inc.

Solomon, Z., Kotler, M., & Mikulincer, M. (1988). Combat-related post-traumatic stress disorder among second-generation Holocaust survivors: Preliminary findings. *American Journal of Psychiatry, 145*, 865-868.

Sorel, E. (2013). *21st Century Global Mental Health.* Burlington, MA: Jones & Bartlett Learning.

Staub, E. (2013). *Overcoming evil.* USA: Oxford University Press.

Stein, N.R., Schorr, Y., Krantz, L., Dickstein, B.D., Solomon, Z., Horesh, D., & Litz, B.T. (2013). The differential impact of terrorism on two Israeli communities. *American Journal of Orthopsychiatry, 83*(4), 528-535.

Steir-Livny, L. (2016). From victims to perpetrators: Cultural representations of the link between the Holocaust and the Israeli-Palestinian conflict. *Interactions: Studies in Communication & Culture, 7*(2), 123-136.

Stevens, M. J. (2007). Orientation to a global psychology. In M. J. Stevens & U. Gielen (Eds). *Toward a global psychology: Theory, research, intervention and pedagogy* (pp. 3-34). Mahwah, NJ: Lawrence Erlbaum Associates.

Stevens, M.J. (2012). Freedom and psychology in the Americas. *Interamerican Journal of Psychology, 46*(3), 205-214.

Straker, G. (2013). Continuous traumatic stress: Personal reflections 25 years on. *Peace and Conflict: Journal of Peace Psychology, 19*(2), 209-217.

Strier, R., & Werner, P. (2016). Tracing stigma in long-term care insurance in Israel: Stakeholders' views of policy implementation. *Journal of Aging & Social Policy, 28*(1), 29-48.

Struch, N., Levav, I., Shereshevsky, Y., Baidani-Auerbach, A., Lachman, M., Daniel, N., & Zehavi, T. (2008). Stigma experienced by persons under psychiatric care. *The Israel Journal of Psychiatry and Related Sciences, 45*(3), 210-218.

Tal, A., Roe, D., & Corrigan, P. (2007). Mental illness stigma in the Israeli context: Deliberations and suggestions. *International Journal of Social Psychiatry, 53*(6), 547-563.

Tarakeshwar, N., Stanton, J., & Pargament, K. I. (2003). Religion: An overlooked dimension in cross-cultural psychology. *Journal of Cross-Cultural Psychology, 34*(4), 377-394.

Tedeschi, R. G., & Calhoun, L. G. (2009). Posttraumatic growth: Conceptual foundations and empirical evidence. *Psychological Inquiry: An International Journal for the Advancement of Psychological Theory, 15*(1), 1-18.

Tennant, C. (2004). Psychological trauma: Psychiatry and the law in conflict. *Australian and New Zealand Journal of Psychiatry, 38*(1), 344-347.

Thabet, A.A., Abed, Y., & Vostanis, P. (2001). Effect of trauma on the mental health of Palestinian children and mothers in the Gaza Strip. *Eastern Mediterranean Health Journal, 7*(3), 413-421.

Tobin, J.S. (2012). Threat assessment: September 2012. *Commentary, 134*(2), 4-5.

Tomlinson, M. & Lund, C. (2012). Why does mental health not get the attention it deserves? An application of the Shiffman and Smith framework. *PLoS Medicine, 9*(2): e1001178.

Turney, D. (2012). A relationship-based approach to engaging involuntary clients: The contribution of recognition theory. *Child & Family Social Work, 17*(2), 149-159.

Tuval-Mashiach, R., & Dekel, R. (2014). Religious meaning-making at the community level: The forced relocation from the Gaza Strip. *Journal of Psychology of Religion and Spirituality, 6*(1), 64-71.

UNRWA (2017). Palestine refugees. *United Nations Relief and Works Agency for Palestine Refugees in the Near East*. Retrieved from https://www.unrwa.org/palestine-refugees.

Van de Mortel, T. F. (2008). Faking it: Social desirability response bias in self-report research. *Australian Journal of Advanced Nursing, 25*(4), 40-48.

Van de Vijver, F. J. R., Chasiotis, A., & Breugelmans, S. M. (2011). A fourfold conceptual framework for cultural and cross-cultural psychology: relativism, construct universalism, repertoire universalism and absolutism. In F.J.R. Van de Vijver, A. Chasiotis, & S.M. Breugelmans, (Eds.), *Fundamental questions in cross-cultural psychology* (pp. 165-189). New York, NY: Cambridge University Press.

Vaughn, L. M. (2010). *Psychology and culture: Thinking, feeling and behaving in global contexts*. New York: Psychology Press.

Vered, S., & Bar-Tal, D. (2014). Routinization of the Israeli-Arab conflict: The perspective of outsiders. *Israel Studies Review, 29*(1), 41-61.

Vishkin, A., Bigman, Y. E., Porat, R., Solak, N., Halperin, E., & Tamir, M. (2016). God rest our hearts: Religiosity and cognitive reappraisal. *Journal of Emotion, 16*(2), 252-262.

Wamser-Nanney, R., & Vanderberg, B.R. (2013). Empirical support for the definition of a complex trauma event in children and adolescents. *Journal of Traumatic Stress, 26*(1), 671-678.

Watters, E. (2010). *Crazy like us: The globalization of the American psyche.* New York: Free Press.

Welfel, E. R., & Khamush, B. K. (2012). Ethical standards, credentialing, and accountability: An international perspective. In M.M. Leach, M.J. Stevens, G. Lindsay, A. Ferrero, & Y. Korkut (Eds.), *The Oxford handbook of international psychological ethics* (pp. 103-112). New York: Oxford University Press.

White, G. (1998). Trauma treatment training for Bosnian and Croatian mental health workers. *American Journal of Orthopsychiatry, 68*(1), 58-62.

Woodbridge, N. (2006). A Biblical critique of the two-fold theory of dispensationalism: The distinction between Israel and the Church. *The Journal of the South African Theological Seminary, 2*(9), 86-109.

World Bank (2018, Jul. 6). Public data: Population. *World Bank.* Retrieved from https://www.google.com/publicdata/explore?ds=d5bncppjof8f9_&met_y=sp_pop_to tl&hl=en&dl=en.

Wright, K.M., Britt, T.W., Bliese, P.D., Adler, A.B., Picchioni, D., & Moore, D. (2011). Insomnia as predictor versus outcome of PTSD and depression among Iraq combat veterans. *Journal of Clinical Psychology, 67*(1), 1240-1258.

Wyshak, G. (2016). Income and subjective well-being: New insights from relatively healthy American women, ages 49-79. *PLoS ONE, 11*(2), 1-16.

Yehuda, R., Schmeidler, J., Giller, E.L., Siever, L.J., & Binder-Byrnes, K. (1998). Relationship between post traumatic stress disorder characteristics of Holocaust survivors and their adult offspring. *American Journal of Psychiatry, 155*, 841-843.

Yom, S., & Saleh, B. (2004). Palestinian suicide bombers: A statistical analysis. *Economists for Peace and Security Newsletter.* Retrieved from http://www.ecaar.org/Newsletter/Nov04/saleh.htm.

Yule, W., Stuvland, R., Baingana, F.K., & Smith, P. (2003). Children in armed conflict. In B.L. Green (Ed), *Trauma Interventions in War and Peace: Prevention, Practice, and Policy* (pp. 242-217). New York, NY: Plenum Publishers.

Zhu, B., Chen, C., Loftus, E.F., He, Q., Chen, C., Lei, X., Lin, C., & Dong, Q. (2012). Brief exposure to misinformation can lead to long-term false memories. *Applied Cognitive Psychology, 26*(1), 301-307.

Zilkha, A. (1992). History of the Israeli-Palestinian conflict. In E.W. Fernea & M.E. Hocking (Eds.), *The struggle for peace: Israelis & Palestinians* (pp. 7-61). Austin, TX: University of Texas Press.

Zuhur, S., Abunimah, A., Malka, H., & Telhami, S. (2008). Hamas and the two-state solution: Villain, victim or missing ingredient? *Middle East Policy, 15*(2), 1-30.

- What is your family name, and is there meaning behind it?

- How long have you lived in this region?

- What is your family religion?

- What is your religion now, and how did you come to faith in it?

- Can you describe your stance on the Israeli-Palestinian Conflict?

- Do you have a problem with your country being at war?

- What do you remember your parents telling you about (Muslims/Jews)?

- Do you have any friends that are (Muslims/Jews)?

- Are you familiar with the (Jewish/Muslim) prophecy regarding Gog and Magog?

- Can you tell me about a time you felt safe?

- Can you tell me about a time you felt scared?

- Do you sometimes dislike a person without knowing much about them?

- Can you describe a traumatic experience you've had?

    - What kind of symptoms followed your trauma?

    - How did you cope with those symptoms?

    - Do you think this event could happen to you again?

- How would you describe (Muslims/Jews)? (e.g., brothers/sisters, enemies, etc.)

- Can you describe a traumatic experience one of your parents had with (Muslims/Jews)?

    - How did this affect you when you heard about this encounter?

    - Do you believe this encounter your parents had has affected the way you view the world?

    - Do you sometimes feel that the events your loved ones faced are going to happen to you?

- Do you avoid putting yourself in situations in which the trauma that happened to your loved ones could happen to you?

- Do you have recurring nightmares of events that have not actually happened to you in real life?

- What sort of events or situations trigger these "memories" or thoughts?

- Do you find yourself more irritable after you think about these things?

- Do you struggle to express to others your feelings about these events?

- Do you feel guilty for not having personally experienced these events your loved ones have?

- When you look at a (Muslim/Jew), do you assume they mean peace or harm towards you?

- Do you feel betrayed by people who have not actually personally betrayed you?

- Describe a negative experience you've had with (Muslims/Jews).

- Describe a positive experience you've had with (Muslims/Jews).

- What keeps you up at night?

- What would you like to say to your enemies?

- If you could change one thing about the world, what would it be?

- Where will you be in 10 years?

- How does the Israeli-Palestinian Conflict end?

- Describe your very earliest childhood memory.

PALESTINIAN ONE

P1 is a 23 year-old male Muslim living in Bethlehem. Though his family identity is Muslim, he dislikes this label because he believes "we are all one." He is not religious. He hates that he is in conflict with Israelis, and has many Jewish friends. He feels betrayed by Arab countries, like Jordan, Syria, Lebanon, and Egypt, who do not support the economically poor people of Palestine. He worries about his future as he wants to get a business degree, but doesn't know how to get it. He is frustrated because he feels like he should have a decent job with all of the work he's put in, but works at a souvenir shop.

P1 has not had an acute traumatic experience, though he has lost sleep in 2005 when Israelis were frequently arresting people around him and destroying homes after the wall was built. He sleeps comfortably now.

P1 does not believe his parents have had trauma.

PALESTINIAN TWO

P2 is a 19 year-old male Muslim living in Bethlehem. He is not religious. He wants peace with Jews to build a united country. He was raised to believe Jews were just like Muslims. He does not have any friends who are Jewish or Israeli.

P2 did not report any trauma.

P2 did not report that his parents have had any trauma.

PALESTINIAN THREE

P3 is a 19 year-old female Muslim studying at Birzeit University in Ramallah, and was originally a refugee from Lod (Nablus). She is religious (and was the only participant who wore a hijab). She has extreme frustration with the Palestinian Authority, who she believes underestimates Palestinians and does not support Palestinians' right to protest. Yet, living under Fatah is better than living under Hamas. She believes Fatah, Hamas, and other Muslim governmental organizations need to cooperate better. She conveyed feelings of hopelessness, saying "you feel like everything you're doing is nothing" in regards to protests, and says she does not fear death because it cannot be worse than what she's already experienced. P3 dislikes social media political posts, saying "words don't matter, actions do."

P3 has endured trauma. This includes being present for gunshots, gas bombs, and helicopters hovering near her, though none of these forces were directed at her. Additionally, when she lived by an Israeli settlement, she had to sometimes lay on the ground in her home because bullets sometimes came through her windows. She claims to not suffer from post-traumatic symptoms, and instead uses this as energy to protest the occupation. She is nervous around checkpoints.

P3's family also has a history of trauma. P3's grandpa was shot in Nablus near his heart, and now "one wrong move could end him." Her dad was also jailed for 10 years by the IDF. She is anxious for her grandpa, and this experience has made her more afraid of the world. She says this is especially true because her grandpa is an innocent man who was shot. This has also made her parents afraid, who forced

P3 to miss a once-in-a-lifetime scholarship opportunity because they did not want their daughter traveling.

PALESTINIAN FOUR

P4 is a 19 year-old male Muslim studying at Birzeit University in Ramallah, and is originally from Ramallah. He is not religious. P4 finds the whole Israeli-Palestinian Conflict "fishy," saying that there seems to be benefit to both Palestine and Israel for engaging in it, as evidenced by the Palestinian Authority jailing their own people when those people have already served jailtime in Israeli prisons. P4 has friends who are Jews, given that they are not Zionists. He avoids politics, protests, and all conflicts. He feels betrayed by the Palestinian Authority for their ineptitude.

P4 did not report any trauma. He does get nervous around checkpoints.

P4 did not report that his parents have had any trauma. His dad was jailed in a case of mistaken identity, but this was quickly cleared up and holds no ill-will towards IDF for this event.

PALESTINIAN FIVE

P5 is a 19 year-old male Muslim studying at Birzeit University in Ramallah, and is originally from Jericho. He is not religious. P5 feels the Palestinian Authority is not doing enough for its people, and wonders if there is a devious cooperation between the PA and the Israeli government. For this reason, he feels betrayed by the PA. P5 is friends with Jews, given they are not Zionists. P5 believes that the Israeli government and PA should be dissolved into a united government that has more accountability, and that the conflict is rooted in the fact that IDF soldiers are scared and too quick to shoot, which causes problems. He believes government cannot be rooted in religion, and for this reason, prefers Fatah (who controls the West Bank) more than Hamas (who controls Gaza).

P5 did not report any trauma. However, he had an event where he wanted to go to the hospital to take care of a physical injury, but did not do so because he didn't feel like being interrogated as if he was a criminal. Checkpoints make him nervous.

P5's grandma and dad have had conflicts with IDF, but he does not know all of the details and does not believe it has shaped his understanding of the conflict in any significant way.

PALESTINIAN SIX

P6 is a 28 year-old female non-Muslim who lives in Bethlehem, and has previously lived in Ramallah and Beit Jala. She was raised Christian, but "believes in all religions" including non-Abrahamic religions, like Buddhism. She does not reject peace with Israel, but says there must also be justice. She identifies much closer to Muslims than Jews, and was raised to be wary of Jews, and says "some [Jews] are without humanity," and adds that she identifies more with Muslims than Jews because "we have stones; they have guns." P6's dad ran a soap factory, and IDF would often steal his merchandise and claim they were doing so because they were collecting on taxes. P6 feels that the Israeli-Palestinian Conflict is exacerbated by Arabs being aggressive and uneducated, and while she believes that it's possible for peace to occur through the Palestinian Authority, she doesn't want to be around to see it and is desperately trying to leave Palestine.

P6 has experienced indirect trauma, mainly through clashes in which shooting occurred. She never knew if Jews or Palestinians were shooting. After these encounters her face would get red and she struggled at school. She was afraid to leave her house, especially when tanks or airplanes were present. She used to hide whenever she heard IDF knocking on doors. Her dad died from cancer, and following this, she would have dreams where he would appear again very sick, and she would ask God to take him away so he isn't suffering. In 2004, she went to a mental health counselor to deal with these symptoms and she feels like it helped, but now she struggles with feelings of insecurity.

P6's father was jailed for not paying taxes when her mother was pregnant with her. P6's mother went into labor with P6 alone (i.e., without her husband) after curfew, and on the way to the hospital, her car broke down. Somebody took her to the hospital. As a result of these experiences, P6 does not want to bring any children into this world and has even gotten into heated arguments with her sister who has a "shallow" mindset for wanting to bring children into the world.

PALESTINIAN SEVEN (Skype interview)

P7 is a 23 year-old male Muslim living in Jericho. He comes from a very religious family but is himself secular. He is tired of the Israeli-Palestinian Conflict and wants everyone to be able to just live their lives. Growing up, he wasn't given any specific warnings about Jews other than to be cautious when having interactions with them. He does not currently have any friends who are Jews. He believes that the Israeli-Palestinian Conflict will be "managed" forever (as opposed to solved) as grudges continue building: he noted that whenever someone suffers a loss, it creates a grudge that is passed down from generation to generation.

P7 did not report any trauma.

P7 reported that he suspects his mother may have had trauma because she randomly lost her sight one day, but she never talks about it.

ISRAELI ONE

I1 is a 29 year-old female Jew living in Jerusalem, and is originally from a settlement. She comes from a religiously orthodox family, but is agnostic and perhaps hostile towards religion. She is somewhat disinterested in the Israeli-Palestinian Conflict because she feels it is largely unsolvable and therefore not worth her attention in comparison to other things she must worry about. She was told to be cautious towards Arabs growing up, and has many personal experiences with Arab men sexually harassing her or her female friends, and as such, finds Arabs to be sexist and intimidating. On the flip side, she believes Jews are inherently racist and don't even realize it, and she notes that "we [referring to Jews] are no better than Arabs" when it comes to the conflict. She adds that the "Jewish people" are very complicated because they are both a religion and a race. She also dislikes discussing the conflict because she feels that nearly every conversation ends with someone inciting the Holocaust, similar to how many American debates end with a political leader being called "Hitler."

Throughout the duration of the interview, I1 claimed to not have any trauma. 3 minutes prior to the interview ending, she suddenly recalled being in Ramallah during New Year's during the Second Intifada and being exposed to gunshots, including one bullet that hit her house. Today, she still gets nervous when an Arab gets on a bus she's riding because she grew up during a period where Arab terrorists frequently blew up busses, and some of her friends' family members were killed during that time.

I1 reported no traumatic experiences to her parents, though she knows that her grandma used to hide under the bed when sirens would go off during the Holocaust. Similarly, a close friend of I1's is petrified of any black-and-white films because the only black-and-white footage she saw growing up were of Jews being tortured in the Holocaust. However, I1 finds these stories interesting only, and says that these instances probably did not shape her worldview. However, it should be noted that I1's brother has become a severe right-wing Zionist (in the political party Lehava), which greatly troubles her because "at 13, he was listening to Backstreet Boys and at 16, he was a religious zealot." This has resulted in her brother being arrested (and appearing at a family bris in chains) and has severed her relationship with him.

During the debriefing period in which I1 was exposed to the true purpose of the study, she noted that the phenomenon of Transgenerational Trauma Transmission does exist, but that researchers will not find the phenomenon as obviously as they would in Gaza, which is where she says the "heart of the conflict" currently is. Additionally, she said that the study itself was much too broad, and that there are too many individual sects of Judaism and Islam that it is too ambitious to study "Israelis and Palestinians" without breaking down their specific cultures. She referenced that Israel is known for a humorous adage that "if you ask 2 Israelis about something, you'll get 3 opinions." Likewise, she says asking a Gaza Arab and an East Jerusalem Arab will completely change the direction of any research study as the East Jerusalem Arab has had peaceful interactions with Israelis, while Gaza Arabs only see Israelis through their scopes.

ISRAELI TWO

I2 is a 32 year-old male Israeli Jew secretly living in Bethlehem, which is illegal under Israeli law and Palestinian Authority. I2 was born in Jerusalem, moved to Atlanta, GA when he was 4, moved back to Jerusalem when he was 22, and has been living in Bethlehem off-and-on for the past 10 years. He was raised in a very religious Jewish family: he hails from some of the most respected rabbinic dynasties, his grandpa created the biggest Orthodox Jewish synagogues in Atlanta, and his dad is currently the leading Orthodox Rabbi of that synagogue. Yet, I2 is not religious and does not believe in a monotheistic god. When asked what he does believe in, he stated, "I believe I exist," but asserted that even that belief was attained after much critical thought. Still, I2 reports that he feels emotionally-connected to his culture and traditions, and is not hostile towards religion. However, he is annoyed towards Muslims in particular for taking Jewish history and altering it so that it fits their own narratives; for example, he believes the only reason that Muslims consider the

Temple Mount a holy place is because the Jews first considered it to be holy. He believes that Arab culture is more rooted in "dramatic effect rather than empirical evidence," and that they view the world in a black-and-white dichotomous lens. Whenever I2 referred to the Jewish race, he used the pronoun "they" instead of "we," and was the only Jew to do so.

When asked about trauma, I2 stated that he is most traumatized by the "stonewall truths that have become decayed" in his life, most notably his Jewish faith, which has led him to distrust institutions and feel betrayed by his parents. I2 discussed how a friend of his blew himself up in 2016, and instead of feeling traumatized by it, he found it to be "like an adventure" and even leaked his friend's family name to the media to use it to his own advantage.

I2 did not report that his parents have had any trauma.

I2 stated that the Israeli-Palestinian Conflict is a "stimulus and response" situation, and that Prime Minister Benjamin Netanyahu simply "taps into Jewish fears" to keep it going, whilst Palestinians actually are devoid of an identity without the conflict. He states that both Israelis and Palestinians actually derive a level of satisfaction from the conflict and especially from "being right," and that the current conflict is an "echo of the original issues." He describes the Israeli-Palestinian Conflict as a brand, that "it's the Red Sox / Yankees rivalry" in which both teams benefit from their dislike for each other. He cites the fact that people now come to Bethlehem to take selfies in front of the barrier wall as a prime example of the conflict becoming like "Disneyland" for both sides. I2 believes that, making matters worse, other countries project their own problems onto the conflict, essentially imagining themselves as participants of the conflict, even when they're clearly not. I2 says that the greatest tragedy today is not the conflict, but the way the Holocaust is used to politicize it. I2 says this is the biggest injustice to the Holocaust victims, and it makes him "sick." I2 expects to be dead in the next 10 years for "trusting the wrong person."

ISRAELI THREE

I3 is a 25 year-old male Israeli living in Jerusalem. He is Jewish by ethnicity but is nonreligious. He worked in the Israeli military as a coordinator between Israelis and Palestinians, and believes that both sides are "stupid" for their roles in contributing to the conflict, and that both Israelis and Palestinians are allowing "nobody trustworthy" to gain political power. He notes that going back to the pre-1967 borders are not an option because if you look at Israel topographically, this would give Arabs a major strategic advantage of height that would put Israel in danger, and that this is why the 1967 war was even possible in the first place. I3 acknowledges that he doesn't have all the facts that the Prime Minister has, but that the Israeli approach to the conflict must change.

I3 reported that he never suffered any trauma, and the closest experience he came to having to deal with trauma was during his military service when he walked into a room full of 30 Palestinians (and no other Israelis), and he could feel the tension in the room. He dealt with this situation by speaking a few sentences that he knew in Arabic, which he said calmed everyone down as he believes speaking in Arabic creates a connection.

I3 reported that his father served in Lebanon during the Second Lebanon War and he suspects he suffered trauma, but it was never spoken of. I3's grandpa had trauma as well and talked about it, but I3 feels it didn't affect him to hear those stories.

During the debriefing period in which I3 was exposed to the true purpose of the study, he noted that he believes trauma is indeed passed down, and remarked that "Jews heal faster" than most people in the world.

ISRAELI FOUR

I4 is a 30 year-old female Israeli living in Jerusalem, and is originally from a settlement. She was raised as a Modern Orthodox Jew and was "very religious" until she was 21 years old, at which time she became an atheist. She states that religion and money are the two engines that run everything in the world. She suffers from clinical depression and takes a combination of SSRIs (citalopram) and anti-anxiety medication (Wellbutrin) now. Growing up, she was told that Arabs are generally liars and thieves as a result of their culture and political leadership. She feels that these are racist sentiments, and describes her dad as racist because "not all Arabs" are deceptive, though she agrees Palestinian leadership is. She believes Palestinians should be given some of their land back, and that she would willingly support her parents and sister losing their land in the West Bank in order to achieve peace. I4 sees Palestinians/Arabs as "cousins." She wishes the world could erase religion and money, but admits she can't even fathom a system where people would work for something other than money.

I4 was in a moderate motorbike accident in Vietnam 5 months ago, and got sick when she stopped antibiotics. Other than this, she did not report any personal trauma, though she says of growing up in the conflict, "it was felt." During periods of attack at school, she remembers the curriculum being shut down and everyone was just supposed to pray because it was too hard to concentrate on school work. Despite the thick tension she grew up in, she said claims her sense of fear is "underdeveloped" and that, growing up, she "trusted in God at that time" and she trusts in the Israeli military now.

I4's grandpa was shot in the leg during the intifada, and she remembers crying when she saw his car have bullet holes. She remembers many conversations began with "did you hear what happened?" in regards to a loved one being harmed in the conflict. She has had teachers and friends killed in the conflict.

ISRAELI FIVE

I5 is a 29 year-old female Jew living in Jerusalem, and is originally from a settlement. She comes from a religiously orthodox family, and is still very religious today. She thinks that economic cooperation would help end the Israeli-Palestinian Conflict but that would require (1) trust and (2) a willingness to lose something, neither of which Israel has. Growing up, it was an unsaid rule to be cautious around Arabs and that they are inherently bad. In religious schools, Jews are taught that Arabs are trying to kill them, but after getting shot at, those lessons don't need to be said anymore. I5 especially has an ingrained fear of Arab men, and stressed that this is passed down intergenerationally. She noted a double standard: Arabs can't whistle at their own women because they might get killed for it, but Arabs have no problem whistling at Jewish women. Additionally, the more recent incidents of Arabs stabbing Jews dictate a need to be cautious around Arabs still. She notes that there are people in the world who are always "trying to make a freier [Yiddish slang for 'chump'] out of you."

I5 did not report any trauma, though did say that she sometimes daydreamed about ways she could die growing up.

I5 reported that she did not believe either of her parents have experienced trauma. She cited that the closest thing to this was when she was young and the sirens would go off, and her parents didn't know where their children all were.

During the debriefing period in which I5 was exposed to the true purpose of the study, she noted that very few Israelis suffer from acute trauma, even during war, but that "it's the day-to-day stuff" that creates trauma (i.e., complex trauma).

ISRAELI SIX

I6 is a 26 year-old male Israeli who has spent his whole life in Israel (currently Jerusalem). He is Jewish by ethnicity but nonreligious. He still respects his Jewish ancestry as Judaism is very important to his mother. I6 is surprised the Israeli-Palestinian Conflict has not been solved yet, and feels that the statehood of Palestine has been ignored too long by Israel. I6 believes that Saddam Hussein was a "vengeful maniac" but that the US made a mistake in killing him, because he was the only one who could control Iraqi Arabs. He said the US is guilty of killing a leader, forcing democracy, and leaving Iraq in shambles. He currently does not have any Muslim friends. When asked how the Israeli-Palestinian Conflict ends, I6 is the only participant who made any reference to the apocalyptic battle of Gog and Magog.

I6 reported no personal trauma, despite claiming that "massive" attacks occurred near his home during the intifada. Even today, he feels there is a "survival instinct" to feel cautious around Arabs.

I6 said scary situations have happened to his parents, but that he doesn't consider them "trauma." He stated "you don't need to look for it [trauma], it'll come to your home." He says that he isn't sure if his parents' scary situations have affected his worldview, though believes it has made him more cautious and he is particularly fearful when he hears Arabic.

ISRAELI SEVEN

I7 is a 26 year-old male Israeli who was raised in Otef Aza, lived in Tel Aviv during adolescence, and moved to Jerusalem 2 years ago. He was raised an Orthodox Jew, but considers himself secular, but tolerates religion. He describes himself as "right-wing but not radical," and states that Israel does not need to apologize for how aggressive it has behaved to protect itself. He was in an elite section of the IDF, and believes that war will break out in Syria, Lebanon, and/or Gaza that requires him to return to service.

I7 does not describe himself as someone who has PTSD, but has experienced what most would consider extensive trauma during his time as a

Paratroop in "Protective Edge" in Gaza. He has had friends who have died. Yet, he states that living in Otef Aza was perhaps more traumatic than his time in the IDF. He was forced to see a military psychologist in a group counseling setting, and he believes this helped him express his emotions and not have any lingering feelings of anger since leaving IDF. Since leaving the IDF, he has joined a security firm, indicating that he still has no problem putting himself in danger. He claims that he is often on edge as a result of his experiences, especially whenever he hears Arabic.

I7's dad served in the Second Lebanon War, but if he faced trauma, it was never discussed because his father internalizes his problems. However, he did sense that his dad was suffering from post-trauma symptoms after the war. I7 did not realize this about his father until his own military experience, which put his dad's behaviors in perspective as a post-traumatic symptom.

I7 believes that some settlements are necessary to keep Palestinian terrorists at bay. He referenced Golan Heights as the best example of why Israel cannot just hand its land over in a peace treaty, citing the 1967 attacks on Israel from enemies in the Golan Heights.

I7 believes that there needs to be a distinction between Gaza Palestinians and West Bank Palestinians. He believes that 90% of Arabs in West Bank (and Jerusalem) want peace and relationships with Israelis, and that West Bank Arabs are essentially Israelis in many senses. As for Gaza Arabs, he feels sorry for them and recognizes that they are suffering. Unlike West Bank Arabs, he has never met a Gaza Arab he wasn't shooting at.

ISRAELI EIGHT

I8 is a 34 year-old male Israeli living in Jerusalem. His mom is a Jewish Afghan immigrant, and his dad is a Czech-Iraqi immigrant. Both parents are religious. I8 himself is a religious Jew, and was the only participant to ceremonially wash his hands before our meal together, and after the meal was done, conducted a 3-minute prayer to thank God for the meal. He believes the Oslo Accords were the "biggest mistake in the entire history of Israel" because inviting the PLO to move from Tunis, Tunisia to Israel and giving them weapons is akin to inviting a rapist to live in your house. I8 says the cultural zeitgeist in Jerusalem is to "enjoy life" while the cultural zeitgeist in Palestine is to "kill people." He believes that Muslim leaders' goals are to keep their followers ignorant of truth. I8 says he will never visit the US because he is insulted when people pull him aside for looking like a terrorist, and he feels that would happen during his travels to the US. I8 believes that the conflict has no end and will be managed forever, adding "Hebrews don't speak Arabic, and Arabs don't speak Hebrew; how are we supposed to talk" about the conflict? I8 has no friends who are Muslim. He wishes he could tell Arabs that the Jewish race is eternal, and that "we were here before you and we'll be here after you."

I8 has been diagnosed with PTSD, and has extensive trauma. He grew up during a time in which he described that riding a bus was like "playing the lottery" as to whether or not it would blow up. He was a tank driver in Gaza during his service which included exposure to rockets, shooting, improvised explosive devices (IEDs), and constant fighting. On one occasion, his unit was hit by sniper fire while he was on the toilet. When he was in Gaza in 2012, he was riding in a military vehicle at

85km/hour when his vehicle hit a bump and he hit his head very hard against a drone screen in front of him. When this happened, tons of traumatic memories came flooding to his mind at that moment, and in particular, one nighttime mission in which he, another enlisted soldier, and one officer were in Gaza. He woke up to a firefight with 3 Palestinians; the officer of the group had prematurely tried to shoot the Palestinians, and his weapon got jammed after one bullet discharged. I8 immediately killed one of the Palestinians, and the other 2 Palestinians began running away. I8 began chasing them, but the officer commanded him to cease the chase. I8 pleaded with the officer to let him kill the other 2, and the officer said he would go to prison if he pursued them. Years later, I8 found out that the officer took credit for killing the 1 Palestinian in order to cover-up for his cowardice and tactical ineptitude. I8 has been to group therapy and engaged in CBT therapy (particularly exposure and response therapy), which has helped him a little bit with going out in public again. However, I8 dislikes being in PTSD groups because he feels like his stories don't compare to other survivors of trauma. I8 frequently has flashbacks of the ambush in Gaza, and he wishes it could have played out differently (i.e., that he could've eliminated the threat). Reminders of this ambush are a source of great stress and pain for him, and often sparks his "dark" days in which he feels depressed, low energy, and emotionally numb. He has never told his parents about his PTSD. On several occasions, he has dialed his mom to tell her that he is struggling, but ends up cancelling the call before it goes through because "once you tell them the truth, they pity you for life." He doesn't want one of his "dark moments" to impact the lighter moments of life in that way, because he believes his mom would be unable to separate discussions about his dark moments with his lighter moments (i.e., she would bring up dark topics when he doesn't want to talk about it). I8 had no traumatic symptoms prior to his military service.

I8 reported that his grandpa was stoned to death in Afghanistan because he was Jewish. I8 reports that this does not affect him from a trauma standpoint, and that in Israel, you can just feel trauma "in the air" anyway. He does not have any specific stories he remembers his parents passing down other than the death of his grandpa. I8 says the trauma is in "the attitudes, not the stories." Specifically, I8 says that when an Israeli is killed in the service of his country, it is a great tragedy for the family; meanwhile in Palestine, mothers are often proud of their sons who commit suicide bombings. I8 acknowledges that not all Palestinians are like this, but that these attitudes have set the tone in Palestine.

I8 adds that there is no reasoning with a group of people who still deny the Holocaust ever happened. I asked him, "Do you believe Palestinians deny the Holocaust?" He told me he didn't need to tell me what he believed and directed me to instead look up the official stance of Mahmoud Abbas, the Palestinian Authority president who was elected by the Palestinian people. I did so, and found that President Abbas does indeed assert that the Holocaust did not happen, and wrote his PhD dissertation on this topic.

ISRAELI NINE

I9 is a 29 year-old female Israeli living in Jerusalem. She is Jewish and considers herself both religious and a nationalist. She says that she believes there is no solution to the Israeli-Palestinian Conflict, and it makes her sad to acknowledge this. She says that she recognizes and sees the Palestinian people suffering, but that

Israel doesn't owe them peace treaties because they have not been partners in the peace process. I9 comes from a right-wing family, and she says her mom is so "extreme" that even calling someone an "Arab" is perceived by her to be derogatory. I9 does not have any friends who are Arab, though has classmates who are and she gets along with them. If she could change one thing about the world, it would be that people at least assess their actions appropriately before doing them.

I9 experienced a traumatic event at 14 years old when a bomb went off near her home (she was not present). The bomb killed 30 people and 3 of her classmates were also injured. This "shattered" her sense of safety and she it made her realize that such an event could happen to her. She lived in a "30 second zone" growing up, which meant that when the alarms went off, she had 30 seconds to get to a bunker before the rocket exploded. She said Jews near Gaza gauge their location in seconds (e.g., "15 seconds zone," "30 seconds zone," "60 seconds zone," etc.) to describe how close they live to the heart of the conflict. These experiences made her grow suspicious of Arabs – especially those traveling alone and with coats or backpacks – when she rode on busses. She suffered nightmares after this, and loud noises – particularly motorcycles – startle her. Additionally, I9 worked on a peace mission in 2006 during the Second Lebanon War and experienced a rocket fly overhead and explode nearby. She said that volunteering on peace missions helps her cope and feel like she isn't helpless in the conflict, and she has found a niche in helping humanitarian organizations translate from Russian to Hebrew. She doesn't like going near the Damascus Gate in the Old City because it's near the Muslim Quarter, where she doesn't feel safe, and she asserts that this feeling is probably true for most Jews. I9 uses dark humor to express her emotions, which she also asserts is common for Jews. I9 sees the conflict continuing on because the Palestinian Authority is "selfish" and that "hating Israel is their focus," and this is evidenced by Gaza receiving significant assistance to develop their community in 2005, and instead of using the funds for building houses or education systems, the Palestinian Authority used the money to build terror tunnels. I9 thinks that a major earthquake is scheduled to come in Palestine near the Jordan River, and that she expects this to change the dynamics of the conflict.

I9 suspects her parents have experienced trauma, but it has not been talked about. Her dad was in the IDF reserves after he immigrated to Israel from Moscow.

ISRAELI TEN

I10 is a 25 year-old male Israeli who has spent his life in Haifa, Tel Aviv, and Amatzia, and only recently moved to Jerusalem. He is Jewish by ethnicity, but his parents were anti-religious: they intentionally disobeyed Jewish customs to be antagonistic to the religion. For example, they would eat pork every Yom Kippur, which is forbidden under Mosaic law. I10 himself is secular, and considers himself to not necessarily be anti-religious. In fact, he is bothered when people (particularly Arabs) try to look at Israel and somehow disregard the Jewish connection to the land. He says he does have empathy for Palestinians, but that Israelis just don't trust them. Today, I10 is friends with "plenty" of Muslims/Arabs. In fact, he says he feels more "connected" with his Arab friends than he would with an American Jew. He does not consider himself as a person who has enemies at all. When asked about a time that he felt scared in life, he genuinely seemed to think hard to come up with an example, but ultimately didn't have any examples to share. He said he remembers one time feeling "anxious" when he was hiking and came to a dead end on a cliff and was short on supplies, but that was the closest he's felt to being scared in his life.

I10 said he did not have any trauma when asked, "just rockets and gunshots" when he was serving in the IDF in Nablus. He was also tasked with finding terror tunnels in Gaza. He says he has never had any posttraumatic symptoms of any kind. Today, he is friends with many Gazans, and he perceives that there is an understanding between them that they can be good friends now, but if/when another conflict erupts in Gaza, they'll have to start trying to kill each other, noting "it's not personal, we're just standing on principles. At least I hope so." Interestingly, I10 expects the IDF (i.e., his own military) to fall to Palestine eventually, and that Israel/Palestine will merge into one country under Palestinian control.

I10 comes from a military family, and says his grandpa was a decorated general who saw lots of combat during conflicts in 1948, 1956, 1967, 1973, and 1982. I10 says his family is unaffected by situations that would be traumatic for others, and cited a story where his grandpa's unit was being bombed, and his grandpa responded in kind by taking a nap. Growing up, his grandpa would laugh at some of these stories, and now I10 has similar stories of his own that he laughs about.

During the debriefing period in which I10 was exposed to the true purpose of the study, he noted that he felt like transgenerational trauma can be found "not in the stories," but the actions of people. He cited the example of his father, who has a fear of heights. He said he didn't learn or inherit his father's fear of heights, but inherited anxiety.

INDEX

* 9 7 8 1 9 3 7 6 9 1 0 7 3 *